May you have a
very happy day
on your birthday

best wishes

James.

TO EVERYTHING
A SEASON

The View from the Fen

'We do not see nature with our eyes, but with our understanding and our hearts.' Hazlitt

For my son, who taught me to look more carefully

TO EVERYTHING A SEASON

The View from the Fen

Charles Moseley

Illustrations by Eric Ravilious

MERLIN UNWIN BOOKS

First published in Great Britain
by Merlin Unwin Books Ltd 2022

Text © C.W.R.D. Moseley 2022
Illustrations by Eric Ravilious

Merlin Unwin Books Ltd
Palmers House
7 Corve Street
Ludlow
Shropshire SY8 1DB
UK

www.merlinunwin.co.uk

ISBN 978 1 913159 36 8

Typeset in 12 point Caslon by Merlin Unwin Books
Printed and bound by CPI Group (UK) Ltd, Croydon

Prologue

I started to write this book before I had any idea, or intention, that it might be a book. In fact, it remains simply what it originally was: a sort of diary cum commonplace book. It is a collection of jottings, impressions, delights, some made decades ago, some just yesterday. So its structure is a sort of kaleidoscope of moments: like the weather, you have to put up with what comes.

All of these jottings reflect my growing and deepening love affair with the countryside of England and its lore, its yearly, seasonal, daily changes, its infinite variety seen even in the dull little spot of earth to which coincidence brought Jenny, my late wife, and me in our morning all those years ago, and where I have stayed till the nights draw in. (It turned out not to be that dull after all.) For as Thomas Gray says in one of his wonderful letters, in March, 1738, 'I don't know how it is, I have a sort of reluctance to leave this place, unamiable as it may seem... [It] is very dirty, & very dull; but I'm like a Cabbage, where I'm stuck, I love to grow...'

But as the notes and jottings accumulated, and poems found by chance were added to the mix, as they turned over in my memory as the unseen ministry of worms turns over the soil, as one file bumped up against another almost forgotten one, they began to take a shape almost on their own, rather like little knobs of butter in milk gradually coalescing as you continue to turn the churn. They came to echo the endless cycle of the seasons, the grave procession of the infinitude of stars across the night sky, the cycle of seedtime and harvest, the languor of summer and the harshness of winter. They came to notate that growing conviction that we human animals cannot thrive mentally or physically when we separate ourselves, by design or chance, from the living, pulsing, infinitely complex interdependent network of what we call, so misleadingly, 'Nature' – as if it were something 'out there.' These jottings came also to be waymarks on that slow, hardly perceived, journey of my own spring into this autumn blessed in so very many ways. *Deo gratias.*

Blessed, not least, in my autumn love, Rosanna Petra.

Autumn

Years ago, I took on a very large allotment on the edge of the village to help make ends meet, for my job (then in publishing) paid little. It was on a bit of good land, where the high land, as we flatteringly call it, slopes down into the levelness of the Fen. It was separated from the Fen by a droveway and a stream – actually, a catchwater drain, dug in the 1600s to stop the little brooks of the spring line going into the fen. For men of substance, the Adventurers, with profit in mind, were trying to drain it.

We grew, my son and I, a small cash crop – wheat, or beet, or barley – and all our own vegetables. Sometimes too many: half a furlong of onions takes some hoeing and there were lots to give away instead of flowers or wine to people who invited us to dinner. (One year the swedes were the embarrassment.) At this time of year, September, there would still be golden days of sun warm enough for me to work there with my shirt off, lifting the maincrop spuds, letting the bits of soil clinging to them dry off while I carried on lifting, and then bagging them for taking home. The onions – and I was always able to grow very good onions, for that land suited them – had been pulled some time back and had been drying off until their stalks were dry, but still flexible. Their shiny gold globes were warm with the sun, and their rustling outer skins, India paper thin, would come off and blow about in any breeze as I plaited the dry stems into long strings. I used to hang them on nails under the eaves of the woodshed where they would catch the sun and air. Soon enough, the drones would be kicked out of my beehives by the busy little ladies getting ready for winter, and their deep-pitched hum would surround the hanging onions where many of them, for some unaccountable reason, always wanted to try to hibernate. Which they cannot do: this is the end of the road, chum: summer's lease does have an end. Coming back along the drove, I used to notice that the trees looked tired, the leaves dull and somewhat ragged after months of weather and photosynthesising. The evenings draw in, and even after a day when I had given my land its first rough digging in the sweat of my brow, I needed to put on a shirt, a sweater, as I walked home. Days grow short and the wind gets a chill when you reach September.

It was – is – easy to see the year as coming to an end, the cycle once more complete, and to indulge in a sort of gentle melancholy. Yet autumn is really a beginning. It is much more than the elegiac fall of the leaf that has reminded so many poets of our own mortality. For in actual fact the year starts here, with getting ready: there is no spring without the dying of the old year into the beginning of new life. As it happens I am in my own autumn, and that is as good a time as any to begin something new: like writing a new book. It has been nudging, pushing, at my mind like the green seedling trying to uncurl itself into leaves, freeing itself from the mould of years past that nourished it. The pressure is at its annoying worst when I am away from my desk – in the middle of the night, say, or out walking in this familiar but ever different countryside where the years have snowed white hairs on me.

The last gale – we have had two corkers recently – has drifted a dark wet wave of dead leaves at the foot of the blackthorns that line the drove. I poke my stick into them – why do I do that? – and stir them, and the layered lower ones are already black with wet and decay. Shining against that dark background is a bright gold acorn. Given a few months, next year's seedlings, the future's trees indeed, will be thrusting greenly through this drift of decay to the strengthening light as the year warms.

Older ages may have marked the turning of the year at the solstice when the sunset begins its northward journey, but you planned the work for your year, bound by the rhythms of field and wood and seedtime and harvest, from the time the swallows left – somewhere between the nights when the Perseid and then the Leonid meteor showers streak the night sky. And when great Orion begins to hunt the Hare across the early night sky you knew that it was high time to kill off and cure your pigs, fat with gorging on the beechmast and acorns of the woodlands and the fallen apples of orchards, and cure them down for the winter. For there would not be much fodder for them after this. Archbishop Ussher of Armagh in the 1650s, following and developing (with great learning and serious calendrical maths) the Rabbinical tradition, calculated everything started in autumn: the world was created at nightfall on Sunday 22 October 4004 BC. His contemporary Dr John Lightfoot, Vice-Chancellor of the University of Cambridge, suggested 9am the next morning as the exact moment. And indeed October has advantages for a beginning, for then the food supply is plentiful and the apples are ripe. (Except that the myth of the forbidden apple is due to a mistake in translation, alas.)

The three Terms – Michaelmas, Hilary (or Lent) and Easter – of the academic year which has structured my professional life begin in October. When the first universities were young, you needed every hand available to get the harvest in before the weather turned, often about the equinox. Then you broke for the long 12 day Christmas feast, then for the spring sowing, and closed the year in time for hay harvest and barley harvest and wheat harvest. For not so very long ago the tides of the countryside lapped up against the life of the town. Michaelmas – the feast of St Michael and all Angels at the end of September – was when agricultural tenancies started, when hands were hired. It is one of the Quarter Days, days for paying rent, settling accounts, starting or finishing tenancies or employment, a day on which in another time I would have been hiring men, or, much more likely, being hired myself as a labourer. Or paying *my* rent, for owning your own house was rare even for the most of the middling sort of people before the 1950s. When we first bought the house where I write this, sixty years ago, it was two 'two up two down' labourer's cottages. In one half as tenants lived Kate and Albert, who had moved in forty years before our arrival and had planted the big double-grafted apple tree that shaded the front of the house until it blew down in a great gale thirty years ago.

Our vendor took us to meet them. 'They're nice' she said, as we slipped through the gap in the hedge that divided the two long gardens, 'and he is an interesting chap: he's been to America.' (As I write that, a sudden memory breaks surface of how big the world used to be.) They lived in the back room, round the Rayburn, tatted rag rugs on the brick floor. Modernisation ran to no more than a single cold tap, a deep pot sink, a single round-pin 15 amp socket, and a light in each room. A tarred corrugated iron privy stood outside, with a bottom-polished wooden seat over the bucket. It was lime-washed inside to keep it sweet, and smelt of Jeyes' Fluid. In the front room, a brown pelmet fringed the mantelpiece of the chocolate-painted fire surround. A line of brass tacks that had once been bright golden held it in place. There was a smell of mothballs and damp. Kate and Albert were, we were told, soon to move to a bungalow close by, and we were offered their house for £500. We did not strictly need the room – two rooms up and two down was already a lot more than we had had before – but, without recognising what the consequences would be over the lengthening years, we agreed. And so in that one morning we had set up the train of events whereby we were soon to be not only householders but also landlords, enjoying a rent of £6.7.6 – just about half my week's income – each Michaelmas and Lady Day.

Youth takes things very lightly, and things don't always sink in. We had been there a month. Michaelmas morning came, a bright clear day with a southerly wind whose warmth was welcome after the chilly night. Kate came through the hedge with her Sunday hat on, a dark blue straw, with her basket, looking important. 'Don't you know what day it is?' she said. 'Friday?' we said, for it was. She looked as impatient as that kind soul ever could, and took from her basket one of her spectacular fruit cakes. 'For you,' she said, 'I always made one for Mrs Shaw [the previous owner] come Michaelmas and Lady Day. Albert will be coming in directly with the rent.' A strange, not altogether pleasant moment. For the Johnsons Michaelmas and Lady Day were days of ceremony, when you put your hat on if you were Kate, for these were the days they paid their rent and ensured their tenancy for another six months. Albert insisted we signed the rent book: our predecessor's signature was there every six months, going back a long way. It was an odd feeling, not easy to get used to. I did not need that legal proof that I could not evict him, for why should I want to?

———•———

The academic year begins, as I said, in October. For decades that cycle has ruled my life, and peasant though I think myself to be, the academy has claims on me I would not have missed. So just when the martins are flying south, arrivals: the first of the wintering geese from the high north, and, from all over, the hopes of the nation, whom one hopes will not be geese. It was always exciting, welcome if quite a shock to the system: first, re-asserting the old patterns and meeting once more colleagues after a long break, when much work had been done, quietly, alone, unobtrusively; and then, students. Some return, like migrants, changed in mind and body by the summer; and a third of them, of course, unknown quantities with unknown qualities and unknown expectations. But it is surprising each year how quickly you shake down into a normality. This is their beginning, this is your resuming.

I remember my own first experience of a Cambridge October – which must be so similar to that of thousands of others. I came up to the University from my Lancashire school with little idea of what to expect and nobody really to advise me. First of all, there was that tense scurry and bustle of trying to pretend you knew what you were doing and, at the same time, feverishly finding out what and who were where and what needed doing *now*, and what could be put off, and trying to get hold of the language and jargon of the place, and all those second and third years with their off-putting confidence... and then the scurry to the Societies' Fair, where various University clubs tried to persuade you to join them, and you did, and then spent the best part of a term trying to get out of all but a few of them.

For someone like me from the damper, cooler and cloudier north, who had only seen Cambridge once before, in the dead December of the previous year when I had come up for a week to take the entrance examination, the weather was – well, the golden light and the balmy temperature made it feel a bit like you imagined Heaven might be on a good day. Nor had I ever been in a place architecturally so beautiful. As often, the first days of Term coincided with a spell of lovely weather, and the river called, and sirens in the second year beckoned you to the languor of punting. Not that I could then do it... but I soon learned, wetly. And so, in all the scurrying, there were some hours of slow progress past the Backs of the Colleges, past mellow old brick, green lawns, golden willows who trailed their soft fingers gracefully in the water, and close encounters with indignant mallard ducks. Then the Upper River called, and, more bold, after taking the College Punt up onto the higher water – the old leat for the long defunct King's Mill – by the rollers next to the sluice, you soon passed into a quieter world, where the banks opened out to green fields, and stands of osiers that once would have been cropped for withies and basket. Then came something approaching wilderness, a place of deep shade under quiet trees, and thick undergrowth, called Paradise. The future seemed such a long way off.

I remember a golden October evening of gentle punting up-river, past where Scudamore's mend their punts, under the Fen Causeway road bridge, then past the (then) mowed lawn of Hodson's Folly on one bank and the Bathing Sheds on the other. Mr Hodson, later butler of Pembroke College, had built the temple-like stone summerhouse in 1887 for his daughter to change in, and from the grass of its discreet, walled, elegant little riverside terrace, Mr Hodson could keep paternal watch on her as she swam in the river. Two matching yew trees flanked the little building. We did not try to make it to Grantchester, for the warm October light was going. We turned by those old pollard willows which Gwen Raverat's wood engravings caught so beautifully in their quietude. Bats were flitting under the lee of the trees of Paradise, taking over from the martins as the dusk deepened. We passed a moored punt, with a couple in it, oblivious to us or the bats. An occasional splash where a large fish turned and broke surface reminded of the life beneath. A bumble bee, I remember, one of the big plump ones, hitched a ride for a hundred yards or so. I hope we were going in the right direction for her.

———•———

As I write, I look out of the study window and my gaze rests on the trees at the bottom of the garden, now beginning to lose their leaves, and I see a jay. I know they are pirates, but they are spectacularly handsome ones, and I do like them despite their guzzling of eggs and small birds when they get the chance. And we owe them a lot, too.

There is an old country saying, 'The thorn is nurse to the oak.' For years it never made sense to me, but by a serendipitous chain of unconnected conversations and reading, it does now. A mature oak produces many, many acorns, and not a one of them has a chance of growing beneath the deep shadow of the parent tree. In season I pick up pockets full of them from the tree I planted decades ago by the river, and I scatter them in places where they might have a chance, where agricultural machinery can't reach and where they will be out of the range of weedkillers. With one exception, that is the last I see of them, but I keep trying. However, the glamorous jay who visits my garden on his raids – actually there may be more than one, but I can't recognise individuals – is the real hero of this story. For the jay in autumn will pick up to nine acorns in its beak or in its gullet and fly off to a bramble thicket or a hedge bottom, often enough hawthorn or blackthorn, where it buries them one by one. In early spring the acorn sprouts, and puts down a strong taproot, while at the same time opening two fleshy leaves full of protein to photosynthesise. Now our clever Jay – I am inclined to give him/her a capital – remembers where he put the acorns a few months back, and does the rounds, and finds succulent protein-rich leaves pushing up to the sun through the leaf litter below the thorns. Just what a hungry bird needs at this thin time of year, and the infant oak with its long taproot can do without the leaves, for there are more where they came from. And so began many of the oaks that once clothed the wildwood country when men were few, and later made our houses, and were shaped into our ships, and so journeyed to the uttermost parts of the earth.

In these parts, come late September/early October, you often get a spell of warm, settled, quiet weather when you could believe that ripe, golden days will never cease: but the dews – some folk still used the old word 'dag' when we first came here – are heavy each morning, and the droplets on the grass blades refract the light of the low sun into spectra to dazzle eyes. It's hard not to have Keats' *Ode to Autumn*, which we 'did' at school without really seeing what it was getting at, constantly coming into your head: lines like

> *...And still more, later flowers for the bees,*
> *Until they think warm days will never cease,*

Which makes me think of when I had my own bees, or the light and the sounds of this season:

While barred clouds bloom the soft-dying day,
And touch the stubble-plains with rosy hue;
Then in a wailful choir the small gnats mourn
Among the river sallows, borne aloft
Or sinking as the light wind lives or dies;
And full-grown lambs loud bleat from hilly bourn;
Hedge-crickets sing; and now with treble soft
The red-breast whistles from a garden-croft;
And gathering swallows twitter in the skies.

He did it better than I ever could: all those sounds I know so well are here in the last verse: first, near, by the river at the bottom of the garden, then, far, from the little rise we call a hill, Will's growing lambs; then the near robin who will follow me round the garden as I do the winter digging, and then the distant swallows making ready to take the summer south with them.

They used to call it St Luke's summer, for his feast falls on the 18th. My bees are working from dawn to dusk gathering the strong-smelling nectar from the ivy tods that overhang their patch of the garden. Their clammy cells will be full of the stuff: pretty well uneatable, in my opinion, but they seem to like it. The swallows are about to go, twittering excitedly, and making momentary crotchets on the telephone and electricity wires. (They space themselves exactly at multiples of their wingspan: so, in simultaneous take-off, no bird will obstruct its neighbour.) A few martins are still about, and the flocking goldfinches are making pigs of themselves on the soft grey fleece of the thistle heads. The low sun is setting noticeably further to the south each day now, and the light is mellow, low across the stubbles where the partridges sit outward-facing in their round coveys. We have no hills here, but I remember Milton's lovely lines – actually, he is remembering his beloved Virgil – about a sunlit evening:

And now the sun had stretched out all the hills,
And now was dropped into the western bay;

Here it is trees that in the golden light reach out across the flat fields to the ditches on the further side. At dusk you can hear the cock pheasants' 'Kek *kek*' as they claim a roost for the night, and let everyone know about it.

Soon, in a month or so, the fieldfares will arrive. The starlings are already performing their evening murmuration. Muntjac deer – little pests – bark their monotonous bark all night: there were none here when we came to this part of England. Hector the Labrador pricks up his ears at the sounds of autumn, and he looks expectant if I go to the gun cabinet. Not yet, chum: let's get a bit of hard weather first. Besides, I have too much to do on the garden getting ready for the next year.

———————•———————

St Luke's Summer, (if we have one), does often end in a gale or two. Thomas Tusser's *Five Hundred Good Points of Husbandry* (1580), reminds us

October good blast,
To blowe the hog mast.

Those October gales bring down the acorn and the beech nuts, the mast on which, until the industrial farming of the last century, pigs from time immemorial were fattened before slaughter – a very good way of harvesting protein from land you could not put under the plough. The pork so fed is delicious. I last ate some in Portugal, where the old ways have not quite given over to industrialised production of meat so bland it could have come off a loom. And now we just waste Nature's bounty.

Poor Tom Tusser, first, miserably, of King's College, Cambridge, then, so happily, of Trinity Hall just along the river. He so desperately wanted to be a farmer, and gave up a well-rewarded, well-patronised career in music – when a treble he was a chorister at St Paul's – to take on a series of tenancies in East Anglia. He was not successful. As Thomas Fuller says in *The Worthies of England* (1662), '[He] spread his bread with all sorts of butter, yet none would stick thereon.' But he left us his book on farming, a sort of Georgic, a mine of useful advice and information about country life in verse that, while it occasionally shows the impress of having read the Greek and Latin poets while at Eton under the formidable Nicholas Udall, can sometimes rise to doggerel. Some people liked it, though: his book went through seven editions, each expanded from the previous, in his last seven years of life. He too begins his book in October, at the beginning of Michaelmas Term, as all agricultural tenancies did: 'a new farmer comes in'.

Jenny, my dear, dead first wife, and I grew up in a part of England where farming even now still means sheep and cows, and only occasionally is a field ploughed for swedes or potatoes. We had never been in a countryside where the soil was black peat instead of stiff clay, where the summer turned most of the land to gold, where combine harvesters crawled across the level fields grazing the corn to stubble. When we came here first, we had never seen before the towers of angry smoke rising into the hot sky from the lines of straw which the machines excreted. For there was no use for the straw, least of all after it was chewed up by the combine, and now the wheat most plant has been bred to have short straw. (Yet up to about 1920, so A. G. Street says in one of his books, a farmer could grow wheat and make his money by selling the long, straight straw for thatching: anything he got for the grain was a bonus.) At night, the long lines of burning straw across the fields lit up the dark, and every so often the bigger heaps where the combines turned sent flames shooting higher into the sky. Beyond question it was beautiful – and enjoyable, both to watch and to light. (I was once in the nick of time to stop my son and an importunate friend setting light to the stubble of our allotment, just combined: there was standing corn for miles, and a merry wind. That sort of memory still makes me curl my toes.) I think we are all closet pyromaniacs, and at harvest time those fires perhaps spoke, like Guy Fawkes' Night, to the sleeping primitive in all of us, who would light his Samhain fires to honour the dead; or just for fun.

You can see it as the ritual threshold of winter, the cleansing; or the stripping for action for the new race to be run. 'Yew gits rid of a terrible lot of weeds that way,' said my friend old Seth as we lit the three rows of straw the combine had left on his little patch of land, and, indeed, you do: Virgil says so as well. Having the land clean of weeds before the next cycle starts is indeed a best foot forward. But Seth was really, I am sure, making an excuse for enjoying it. Once, my parents were making their first visit to us from Lancashire, just after harvest. We had finished the meal, and the gathered dusk invited a quiet smoke outside. The northern horizon was ringed with stubble fires. And my mother suddenly shudders: 'It's just like the Blitz' – for to her this brought back with unexpected intensity the year I was born, the nights of bombing and terror and dogged determination in Manchester. And my father reminds her of her aged mother, born when Victoria had only just lost her Albert, standing in the garden in Fallowfield refusing to enter the Anderson shelter –'not just yet' – looking north at Manchester burning, and saying to him, 'O Tom, isn't it beautiful!' Sometimes the old see things differently.

Sometimes, though, in a dry year, the fires took hold on the peat itself, and might even find a piece of oak lurking beneath the surface, dry enough to take fire and smoulder. If it was a really big trunk, the fire could eat its way in for yards under the soil, almost unseen: no flame, no smoke, only a pervading bitter-sweetness that could be smelt on the wind two fields away – and steam when the rains of October started. Once 'pitted in', a big fen fire would burn for weeks, months even, and some would not die until they had burned themselves right out, or a big snowfall came to smother them. To try to put them out, to dig them out, might only make things worse by increasing the supply of air to the fire. And so the fire down below burned, and those who knew trod warily round it. For not seldom, the surface of the land would look as if nothing was amiss, yet it was a thin crust over the furnace. Men, and animals, had been known to fall in: then the sudden rush of air lets the pent-up gas explode with a blue flash and a 'whoosh': and a scream.

It does not happen now: or not much. Stubble burning was stopped two decades ago. The last fen fire I saw was caused by a group of youths, joyriding in a stolen car, and then abandoning and firing it. As luck would have it, under the ground where they left the car there was a buried bog oak. It burned for weeks.

In those years when people did not plough the land immediately after harvest, as most do now, the stubbles had another benefit particularly appreciated by connoisseurs. Grain dropped by the combine – they are not all that efficient – sprouted, and brought the wild creatures – the wintering duck, and pheasants, and partridges – to feed on it, and dinners to a man with a gun. But, also, field mushrooms, and puffballs, and inky caps, grew in profusion then. If the lines of straw were burned, so much the better, for then the pale mushrooms could easily be seen, no longer covered by straw. Thus was an autumn pleasure made much easier. You could in half an hour gather a couple of two gallon buckets, full; the pleasure in simple gathering way beyond need or even use is I suppose a very atavistic pleasure. We ate them; we preserved them; we gave them away to other people who probably had gathered more than enough of their own. My friend Seth taught me on which fields they usually grew. Sometimes they stood up proud of the soil, clear against its blackness, and some would be six or seven inches across. But those are the easy ones: Seth taught me how to walk across a field that was apparently bare of them and go unerringly to where great clusters lurked in their velvet secrecy just under the soil. You looked for the little radiating cracks in the black soil, as if something were about to break through – as indeed it was. It is a trick I mastered well, and it annoyed the family so much that a suggestion we go mushrooming nearly always brought refusal – even though they liked mushrooms. I could walk in their footsteps and fill a bucket with what they had missed. But we did get somewhat fed up with mushroom this and mushroom that by the time the first frosts came and finished them off.

An old story of Seth's: 'Dew yew knaow why those old mushrooms grows in circles?' We begin to explain that we do, but we are stopped. 'Nar. . . yew knaow mushrooms only grows where there used t'be 'orses? Well then, them mushrooms, they grow where the stallion used to piss, and when he finished, he shook his pizzel about, and the drips, they fly in a circle wun't they? and that's where yew'll find mushrooms.' God bless stallions.

There are few mushrooms now, and none on what were the very best fields. For those were bought by a man who called himself a farmer, and he put them down to turf. Which he literally mined. The best soil in England was shaved off with its covering of a single species of grass, for golf courses, and suburban gardens, and other merely decorative things. And to get turf to that exacting quality he soaked the land in fungicide and pesticide and every other sort of –cide, and nothing grew save uneatable grass, and the land stank of chemicals. Then, when he had exhausted the black soil, he sold the land to the National Trust. I can't remember his name, but I do remember his dog was nice.

———————•———————

We have in the garden several varieties of apple. I planted all the trees, for when we came there were only two. In the back garden, there was a Prince Albert, a cooking variety that stores exceptionally well – and that mattered to country folk in the old economy. In front of the house was old Albert's double-grafted tree, which delivered each year oodles of small yellow apples, of two varieties, one excessively sour, and the other at the right moment almost too sweet. Neither stored, and I suppose we should have made cider with a mix of them both. The old folk would have done. As it happened, most of the time, to my shame (now) we left them to lie. But they were not quite wasted, for Ernie's milking cows, as they came up the lane morning and evening, would make a beeline for them and guzzle them until they were moved on by 'Gir up there!' from Ernie or his pretty daughter, and what the cows left, and what they trod, was a feast for the blackbirds and the wasps. And the cows left very large odorous traces of their slow, deliberate progress, which I would shovel up into a bucket and strengthen the virtue of the compost heap of which I was getting to be quite proud.

That tree blew down, eventually, and the wonderful Prince Albert was a very poor old gentleman when we arrived, long past his peak. He was hollow from broken top – he had lost his crown a few years back, old Albert said, in a March gale – to bottom. His gnarled bark was home to many insects, and a yaffle, a blur of scarlet and green, was occasionally and spectacularly seen drilling into the wood. Inside, year after year there was a family of blue tits. We never knew whether they were related to each other, one of the young coming back to where the brood had been hatched. I suspect so. But one year I found the cat that had adopted us – a Manx of dubious morals, some beauty, and infinite if insincere charm – scooping the half-grown nestlings out one by one with her paw and eating them like humbugs. There were no more blue tits there the next year, which suggests my theory of a family home might have been right.

But we needed more fruit. So in went a Bramley Seedling, two Cox's Orange Pippins, an Egremont Russet, a Blenheim Orange, and a James Greaves. The James Greaves is ripe in late August, and is a wonderful pollinator for other trees. Its apples are, I think, worth eating until late September, but after then you might as well waste your money buying rubbish like Golden Delicious from France in the supermarket. (We grow wonderful apples in Britain: why buy in poorer stuff from abroad?) By late September, the Blenheim, the big apples of which you can either eat or cook, is ready, and so are the Russets, with their delicate aroma of almond. They are wonderful apples for up to Christmas. In October you are gathering and storing the plump, waxy-skinned, pink-flushing Bramleys. They are not the peerless, lamented, Prince Albert, but are fine cookers and they will keep until April. If you do keep them till then, they have changed their nature: from being the slightly tart classic cooker, with the turning of the year they have become delicate sweet eaters. Also, October brings the incomparable Cox's. You know they are ripe when you shake them and you can hear the pips rattle. Well stored, they will keep till a good time after Christmas, and though they lose their first crispness, they never quite lose that scent of late autumn.

But there was – is – also a nameless tree that self-set in the hedge. All named apples are grafted, for they do not breed true, and if a tree grows from a pip, as they will, you have no idea what you are going to get. This tree grew hardly noticed until suddenly one spring there was a riot of the rose-flushed buds that precede the white blossom. I have no idea what it is, and experts I have asked have no idea either. The first year it fruited abundantly, we did not bother to gather the fruit. A first, experimental, bite into the shapely hard fruit revealed only bitterness that did not even promise good cooking qualities. But how wrong… The fruit of this most unusual tree is not worth touching till January. Then, quite suddenly, it mellows into the delectable, long lasting sweetness that can still grace our table in early April. So now that has to be stored too: what was the stable – my son and I built it – is filled with box upon box of apples each autumn, which have to be stacked with all sorts of ingenious devices to stop the equal ingenuity of the field mice who move in when the first cold evenings and frosts arrive. I would not mind so much if they would finish one apple before they start on another.

One thing leads to another. Nature's bounty – well, it would be churlish not to pick the abundance of the sloes in the hedges, shiny and black when your fingers rub the misty bloom off them. It would be such a waste not to harvest the blackberries, or the wild plums that go quite well with casseroled pheasant, or with spices and time turn a cheap gin into something rich and strange. You may have a freezer full of last year's, but no matter: the compulsion is strong. So with apples – all those windfalls! Well, the wasps clean up some, and the blackbirds more, and I always leave a goodly number in among the fallen leaves which I know the birds will find useful when things get tight. But the others… a juicer and a press are the answer. Gallon after gallon of the juice is squeezed from the pulp into a big polythene barrel, and within minutes the creamy white of the foam has turned brown. You leave it two days, and the sediment settles, and you can rack off a clear golden liquid, not yet fermenting, into plastic bottles and clap them into the bigger freezer that has become an essential. That apple juice, unfrozen to need, is no bad consolation for the unfortunate who has to avoid the wine at table in order to drive home. Of course, an earlier time would have let the juice ferment, and made a sharp dry cider… just what we, in our youthful ignorance, never knew to do with the little apples from Albert's double-grafted tree.

It felt right, in an oddly mysterious way, to be planting those trees, watching over their growth. For homes need the blessing of fruit. You cannot escape the myths all peoples who live where apples grow weave round them. Apples are immortality, and death: sweet flesh, but cyanide at the core. They are a druid's wand of power. They are a bang on the head which sends knowing the universe into free fall. They are a gift at a wedding feast that leads to endless war. They keep the gods of the cold north alive. An apple was the first theft, the first crime, a happy windfall.

Ne hadde the appil take ben,
the appil taken ben,
Ne hadde never our lady
a ben hevene quen

Blyssid be the tyme
that appil take was!
Therefore we mown syngyn
Deo gratias

———— • ————

My neighbour has a fine Victoria plum tree, which usually crops heavily. Those plums I like almost as much as greengages, but greengages are shy things, and so often – but less so now, with the heating of our world – the blossom gets cut by a late frost. Paul lets me pick his plums, and timing is everything. A day too soon, and they are bullet hard and sourish. A day too late, and the wasps have moved in, gorging on the dripping sweetness of their juice. Sometimes the beige and mauve of the skins has a dark purple patch: you know that that fruit has the caterpillars of a fruit moth inside, and there will be a tiny hole in the skin where the gummy juice has oozed and set into a little hard bright globe of sugar. But there are enough to go round, and why should not the wild creatures have their share?

Just as I loved keeping bees, so I feel kindly towards wasps. I admire the tenacity with which they will shave bits off the teak garden chairs to masticate into paper for their nests; I respect the determination with which the over-wintered queens will search out a suitable nesting site; and I am in awe at the architecture of the nests, starting with a few small spirally set cells in a globe often suspended from a beam, say, in the loft, and growing into a great city. The largest I ever saw was in our roof: a foot high, and eighteen inches wide. They do not bother us much, except in August and early September when they want to share lunch in the garden. Moreover, their catholic taste extends not only to smoked salmon and avocado, but to dead things that rot, and overripe fruit, and all the things that need clearing up and cycling back into the pattern of growth and maturity and decay. As with spiders, which some folk find difficult to love, they make life on this planet possible for us humans.

Fall of the leaf; and I can't ever forget the unfolding in the 1960s of the slow catastrophe of elm disease, all of us helplessly watching it, grieving. That changed for ever the loved landscape of lowland England...

The green elm with the one great bough of gold
Lets leaves into the grass slip, one by one, –
The short hill grass, the mushrooms small milk-white,
Harebell and scabious and tormentil,
That blackberry and gorse, in dew and sun,
Bow down to; and the wind travels too light
To shake the fallen birch leaves from the fern;
The gossamers wander at their own will.
At heavier steps than birds' the squirrels scold.
The rich scene has grown fresh again and new
As spring and to the touch is not more cool

Than it is warm to the gaze; and now I might
As happy be as earth is beautiful,
Were I some other or with earth could turn
In alternation of violet and rose,
Harebell and snowdrop, at their season due,
And gorse that has no time not to be gay.
But if this be not happiness, – who knows?
Some day I shall think this a happy day,
And this mood by the name of melancholy
Shall no more blackened and obscured be.

Edward Thomas

As soon as the clocks go back, we used to say, the spiders move in. To be sure, it is not all of them, or all 650 varieties of British ones. The big speckled ones, with bodies as big sometimes as an old shilling, (*Areneus diadematus*) who string strong webs between the two clipped yew bushes outside the study door, and sit in the middle shaking them if they sense movement nearby, they don't come in. But the big Wolf spiders – you can listen to their mating song on the Web (appropriately enough!) – come in, and the Giant House Spiders (*Tegenaria duellica*), who can be three inches across, arrive and make themselves at home. They rustle as they move across wallpaper. Sometimes they get stuck in the empty bath, where they probably went because they smelt water in the drain, and have to be helped out. For I don't like killing them. Nor do I particularly like handling the big ones. And not everyone likes them in the guest bedroom.

We had a lady of a somewhat nervous disposition staying once, and in the middle of the night she woke us with a shriek. Ready for any intruder, and grasping (but not drawing) the sword that lives in our bedroom, I went to her lit room next to ours and threw the door open. From a mound of bedclothes on the bed a muffled voice sobbed, 'Get him out! Get him out!' There was no man to be seen, though the easily accessible window was open. Then one realised. On the ceiling directly above where she lay was a perfectly peaceable Giant House Spider. I said, 'But it's a lady, not a gentleman.' 'I don't care, get it out!' Well, we did, in the end, though they can move surprisingly fast. Our friend is still our friend, but comes rarely.

So how do you stop them coming in? One trick which, I have been told, works is to take bright shiny horse chestnuts and put them on the windowsills. The scent, some say, deters arachnid visitors. Others, more sceptical of any chance of keeping them out, say that the nuts must be shiny so the spiders can see themselves mirrored in them, and be frightened off. Some say eucalyptus oil puts them off. But that makes the cure seem worse than the disease. Who would want to live in a perpetual smell of cough sweets?

Other visitors make themselves at home at this time. The devil's coach horse beetle is welcome, for he (or she) comes and eats up the silverfish that are in any old house. Once a cricket sang all winter by the hearth whenever we put a fire on – but that was at a time when we could still expect to see glowworms (not worms at all, but beetles) of a summer night by the river at the bottom of the garden. Pesticides have got rid of those delights. And there are the queen wasps, looking and usually finding ingenious and unexpected places to sleep the winter away. And last of all, when things get cold, the big-eyed field mice. It is so difficult not to welcome such pretty creatures, but...

In other ages when times were hard you kept your cat hungry to make sure it did its job of eating such wasters up. We had one, the prolific Manx. She gobbled up spiders, crunching them with gusto, sometimes leaving a leg behind.

————●—

Autumn – say late October, or early November if it stayed warm – was when I used to put the bees to bed. They don't hibernate, just go into a sort of tick-over, and gather in a dense mass in the middle of their hive, and take it in turns to be on the cold outside of the conglomeration. So on a warm day when the workers would still be foraging in the ivy, I used to open the hives, take out the zinc queen excluders, check that there was no sign of wax moth in the crannies of the frames and hive – a bad infestation can wreck a hive – and, most importantly, that they had enough supplies stored in their combs for the winter and to get them going in the spring, and if they had not, I fed them with sugar syrup. Then I put the hive back together, made sure it was weathertight, put a brick on the roof to stop it blowing off, and hoped for the next season. I loved my bees.

But now, as everyone knows, bees are in trouble worldwide. It is almost an event, now, to see a bee foraging in the lilac-coloured flowers of the rosemary in the back garden in early spring. Even only ten years ago the bush would be loud with their busyness when the early spring sun rose over the roof of the house and touched its pale flowers with glory, and the bees would be loud and late to bed as the last rays of the autumn sun gilded the yellow stamens of the ivy flowers. There is even silly talk of making robot bees – as if the solution is not staring us in the face: stop spraying the poisons on our crops, even if the big firms like Monsanto, now bought by Bayer, or Syngenta, or DowDupont, who are *of course* to be trusted, keep reassuring us that there is *no* risk *whatsoever*. None at all... So why do farmers when spraying have to wear protective clothing? I sign many petitions and write to MPs about the latest ever-so-necessary devilry like the neo-nicotinoids, but all the protest and all the science seems to be ignored. All seems hopeless. For not only bees but most insects are in trouble worldwide. And on the insects depends so much of the pollination of the fruits and crops on which we depend.

William Cobbett, with whose sometimes cantankerous views I find it easier and easier to sympathise, was, according to G. K. Chesterton, the 'noblest English example of the noble calling of the agitator.' He cared passionately about what wholesale Enclosure of the common land was doing to the English peasant; deplored, long before Ruskin, the sprawl of the new industrial towns and their polluting factories over the good, sweet land of England; and hoped that with good instruction the rural poor, and even those not so poor, could be taught to use what resources they had and to manage their economy so that they had a healthy and fulfilled life. He would have been incandescent about the irresponsibility of Big Pharma and Big Agriculture. He would have been appalled at the unthinking, obscene, wastefulness accepted in our society, even – perhaps worst – by those who can least afford it at the bottom of the heap.

In 1821-2 he published seven pamphlets (collected into a book in late 1822) called *Cottage Economy* – he explains the perhaps unfamiliar word on the first page – for 'the Labouring Classes of this Kingdom.' I wish I had known to read him all those years back as we innocents began our own tentative attempt to be as near self-sufficient as we could be. His pamphlets give good advice: Brewing Beer (did that, for years), Making Bread (still do, with organic flour ground by the windmill in the next village), Keeping Cows (if only!) Keeping Pigs (she said if I got a pig she would leave,) and so on, from the keeping of poultry (we did ducks, geese and hens) to candles and rushes, mustard, dress and household goods, fuel, hops and yeast, making and using an icehouse – right down to an addition by Mrs Cobbett on mangel-wurzels and the use of what we call maize and they called Indian corn. He begins pamphlet no. VII with recommendations for the keeping and management of bees.

Bees were once in pretty well every cottage garden early in the last century. Their wax gave polish, and candles for high days and holidays (before paraffin, the poor would use smoky rushlights or smelly tallow dips), their propolis gave a strong, wonderfully scented glue and could be made into an ointment for wounds, their honey made mead and sweetened the sour hardness of a life on the land. In the village we came to there were people who could remember such a time, and they did not wish it back. But several people still had their beehives, and, of course, one had to try…

There was a time – not quite ten years – when this garden, just under two roods or perches in area, was busy. There was a horse in the stable, a large vegetable patch, hens guzzling the scraps we boiled up with some meal for them (as well as foraging for themselves), ducks on the river, geese in next door's orchard, and four beehives which were my pride and joy. One winter my neighbour Colin Washtell had given me an old hive, which I cleaned up, anticipating his promise of a swarm from his hives the next summer – and one came. And then I got more hives, and my own hives swarmed, and then a strange swarm of different race came and hung their humming mass just four feet from the ground under a low branch of the chestnut tree. That evening my ten-year-old son spoke to me on the phone – I was away on business – and with a diffidence that revealed his pride, said, 'We had a swarm arrive, but it's all right, I took and hived them.' And he had: a good swarm, who gave us nearly 100lbs of honey that season.

You get fond of bees, though it is never wise not to treat them with respect. They are not cuddly, as fowls can be. I loved their busy fumbling of the fruit blossom, I admired the strictness of their economy and the cleanliness of the hives, but when the last colony died with the advent of the awful varroa disease, I did not replace them. We were after all, an empty nest by then, and that chapter had closed. But I have missed them, and I think my fruit crops have been less in the bee-less years.

———————◆●———————

Up to yesterday this has been a very quiet autumn, a sustained high pressure system giving us warm days in the soft light of the post-equinox sun, and a generous dew at night so that the Green showed the paths of every early riser and dog walker who had crossed it. Most of the browning leaves, looking tired, still clothed many of the trees, like a worn out dress on a woman fallen on hard times. By chance I came across, one of those golden days, Edward Snow's translation of a poem by Rainer Maria Rilke:

> *Lord: it is time. Your summer was superb.*
> *Lay your shadow on the sundials*
> *and in the meadows let the winds go free.*
>
> *Command the last fruits to be full;*
> *give them only two more southern days,*
> *urge them to completeness, and chase*
> *the last sweetness into the heavy wine.*

It is time. First hint of a change was a thickening of the light, a loss of sharp contrast, and a veil of high cloud approaching from over Ely way. Then little erratic flaws of wind began to gather the leaves that had fallen in the lee of walls and tree trunks, and outside our back door where the wild plum still held a few of its sour fruit. Little swirls of leaves rose and fell back. Then the flaws became a breeze, noticeably cool, that settled in the north east – the coldest quarter for this house, for on that side I planted no windbreak years back because it would have killed our view. Down the lane, which funnelled the wind, a wind more confident was soon dragging its feet in the accumulating dead leaves, as I loved to do when a child: who had been told not to.

The strengthening wind soon began to break the last hold the leaves had on the branches, and the note of its roar changed as the trees became naked. The drooping golden branches of the weeping willow by the river were soon flying out almost horizontal. The river's tent was broken. A plastic bucket clattered off the garden table. The yew down the garden sang its gale song, a steady note, about A. On the river's surface a miniature swell was developing, lines regularly following each other as if on a miniature ocean as the energy of the wind met the resilient friction of the surface. Jackdaws tumbled home to their roosts. It would be a big wind, and the last of summer was over.

I was not quite accurate when I said we had no windbreak to the north east. We had a sort of one: an ancient plum tree on the river bank that did not spoil the view. It gave little fruit, looked a mess when the leaves had gone, but was left because – well, it was there, and getting it down would have probably meant dropping it into the river, with all the problem of getting the large bits out and up the bank. One north-easterly January gale, with snow, did bring it over, but in a sort of half-hearted fashion. Its roots on the river bank had given way, but there was still a firm grasp of the ground on its other side. The tree leaned on its elbows, so to speak, in a most inconvenient position and place, on the edge of the lawn, almost squashing the perfectly well-behaved young Bramley apple. What to do? This was long before we could afford a chainsaw, and getting it to bits would have been one hell of a job, made a lot of mess and seriously damaged the suffering Bramley. So… an old ship's rope I had picked up on the beach in Norfolk, a chain round the thick branch now uppermost, and I waded across the little river – damn cold! – carrying the end of the rope to the bottom of the high bank. Then, having led the rope through a block tied to a tree, we heave, and the ugly plum tree is nearly, not quite, as upright as it was before. And it stands on its own, balanced so that, as you might say, a puff of wind would blow it over. So I ran round and propped it with some old scaffolding planks, and in the next few weeks gave it a serious haircut to reduce the top hamper. As I write, 30 years later, it still stands, clearly now a very old and tired tree, but still snowing white petals below it each spring.

In 1987 there was the biggest wind I have ever known. Comparisons were made by the historically minded with the Great Gale of 1703, which sank so many ships – and half the Navy in the Downs. There those ships still lie, buried in the sands ground out of the soft coast by the tireless tides and brought down from mountains far away by the majestic rivers that flow into the Narrow Seas. Every so often they see the light of day again, uncovered for a space at low tide as the sandbanks of that treacherous coast shift, and then cover them again. The 1987 autumn gale came on October 15 after a dry summer, when all the trees were still in leaf, and their spreading roots were in ground almost bone dry, with little adhesion. After that tumultuous night, we walked down Trumpington Street in Cambridge to see a huge bough twisted off a big horse chestnut lying in the road outside the Fitzwilliam Museum. One of the neo-Gothic crockets on the tower of the Pitt Building in which I used to work had crashed down into the road. Dozens of trees were snapped off. Not one train ran between Cambridge and London. Settling to work was a fidgety business: there was so much one wanted to know and see. The enduring memory of that gale is driving to beloved Felbrigg Hall that weekend. Dear friends had retired there. On the way, first we saw the still full-leaved avenue of beeches just before Newmarket Heath all felled, all felled, by the big wind. Then, turning into the Hall's drive, grief... Along it, before he died, Robert Ketton-Cremer, a man who passionately loved Felbrigg and its sandy land, its lapwing-loud Great Field and the trees of the Great Wood, had planted an avenue of oaks. Compared to the gnarled old folk deep in the woods which had watched seasons come and go and kings and princes and the great ones of the earth wear out their temporary glory into dust, they were striplings – a mere fifty years old, a handful of feet in girth. But their youth was lovely, graceful, deserving of the lissom dryads in whom I could almost believe. All down, all down, their leaves already withering. A future that would not happen.

But. There is always a but. As Oliver Rackham was swift to point out in one of those books that has most influenced my thinking about the dynamic countryside, a fallen tree is an opportunity. Where the light can now reach, plants long dormant can grow and breed, and the insects that feed on them can have a field day. In the end, saplings will grow, and one day trees will once more shade out the full sun with their sounding canopy. The fallen trees are useful, a boon, to man and beast and insect and plant: few habitats are as rich as a rotting oak. There is no such thing as waste. Every end is a beginning, every beginning an end.

'Did you see that ice on those old puddles this morning?' said Albert to me as I went to get the car to go to work. 'Hard weather coming, sure of that. This warm spell won't last.' Well, all country folk are pessimists – I am myself. The land is too dry, or it is too wet. It's too cold for the seeds to germinate, or it's too hot, and things will never come well. Charles Benham, who wrote some enjoyable verse in the speech of his native Essex, put it well:

There's olluz summat. When tha's wet
The corn git laïd, the häy git sp'iled
And when tha's dry the lan' git set.
That fare to make me wholly riled.

We get through, on the whole. But that early, thin, ice glinting in the sun was real enough, and a reminder to gather the last of the runner beans when I got home that evening, in the last of the light evenings. (I always set runners late, so that we don't have a glut of dwarf beans and of runners at the same time.) They freeze well – so much easier than salting them down, as we used to, in big gallon glass jars that had once held sweets.

───────●───────

One of the biggest changes in this village in my decades here has been the wood. Once upon a time every parish had its wood – some still do – where pigs could be run to fatten on the acorns, and timber for wall and roof, tool and cart could grow, and the poor could gather sticks and small timber to kindle their fire. But this was a pretty treeless area, and people need trees, whether they know it or not. The top of the hill for over a thousand years had been quarried for building stone, and as the quarrying ceased, acre upon undulating acre went back to farming. It was always poor thirsty stuff to grow things on, drying white and hard as concrete most summers and most winters wet and slippery as axle grease. It came up for sale – and the village raised the money, and the support from outside, to buy and plant it with trees. There were those in the village, to be fair, who resisted mightily, feeling it was stupid or worse to rewild land that was under the plough. For men and women who had made their living from the hard slog of farming and who remembered times when people went hungry, I can understand that. No consensus is ever solid.

Even so, one blustery, damp November Saturday, with damp scudding cloud threatening yet another shower, a ragtag and bobtail of people of all ages, colours and backgrounds turned up to plant trees, little whips of no more than three feet, if that: 3,200 that first day. We planted randomly – we grabbed twenty or thirty whips each at a time, jumbled them all up, and planted them in no sort of pattern, leaving only the marked-out sinuous rides clear. It was a happy day of putting something right, and people went home cheerful, feeling something had been shared. And so indeed it had: with folk yet unborn who might sit under the rustling shade of those trees of a summer evening.

I was on one of my regular autumn visits up north, and once again was standing on a hillside in what used to be (and still is, for us who grew up knowing the loved old names and identities of the ancient shires of England) Westmorland – the Western Moor Land. They call it Cumbria now: a neither fish nor fowl name that has the single merit of reminding us that here was once the territory of the Welsh-speaking Cymry. I know this patch very well: in fact I think of it as my home patch, long exiled though I have been in the south, and I return time and again like a homing bird. An honorary uncle of mine was Vicar of a parish in the next valley that leads to Kendal, and I have known this dale since I caught my first trout in the bend of the river below where I stand on this clear cold day. It was only a small one: and my father's rod was not a proper trout rod, but I can still remember the physical thrill, the sudden going up a gear, as it took my fly in the pool below the rapid at Rigmaden with an energy that astonished a boy used to the more stolid (if larger) fish he caught off Blackpool's North Pier. Life-changing.

High above me two watchful buzzards mew to each other as they spread their primary feathers to finger the wind, and scribe their irregular ellipses in the sky. A cock pheasant calls from the covert below me. A stream runs through that wood to join the Lune, and in season sea trout make their way up almost to the trickles at the edge of the moor to spawn. I found an exhausted cock fish once up there, the water too shallow to cover his back, and gently lifted him and carried him down to a deeper pool. I hope he made it back to the sea, and food. But he would be one of the lucky ones if he did.

I love this land. I love its cycles of being, year on year, in all their rawness – for the life of the fields and moors is not a pretty, cosy thing, but tough and costly. The cycle of life *is* costly. The sea trout often die when they have spawned; pretty little lambs can die of cold, or their ewe's neglect, or get fly strike from the green-backed flies in summer, or fall to a fox's stealth as the spring evening softens to dusk. The flies' maggots literally eat them alive. The carrion crows wait to peck out the eyes of dead sheep or rabbits, or stranded lambs. But getting to know a patch of countryside really well over many years in all its sunny and dark moods – well, it deepens and changes as you yourself change, coloured by memory, by increasing knowledge and understanding of how it worked, and works – and by acceptance that suffering and death are as natural and necessary to us as birth and the happy couple's love as they sit under the apple blossom in the farm garden. For what our urban-dominated mindset calls merely 'countryside' is a dynamic place, a palimpsest of memory and human experience. That is true anywhere.

In this valley people have lived, worked, loved, died, since hunters first followed the animals who moved north into the new tundra as the Great Ice retreated. They have left their marks and memory. From where I stand on this hillside I can look west across the valley and see the moraine dumps the last glacier left, cut through by the then more vigorous Lune. Once it was a violent, overmastering, meltwater river draining the water melting from the little relic icecap left on the Howgills, carving through the rocks of the earth as if they were butter. Even then men would have hunted here, preying on the herds of reindeer that grazed on the colonising lichens and mosses. You can see people's traces too: the westering sun, when it is low, picks up and shadows round the ghosts of farmsteads that date back to the Iron Age, if not before. They are barely perceptible as you walk over them save in the odd patch of greener grass, and in the ghosts you think you can hear keening in the wind. The lines of the stone walls that net down the heaving of the hills – well, some of those may well go back to the very first Neolithic farmers who came to tame this land; some are a few centuries old, merely. And many of the sites where sit the modern white farms, which visitors love to photograph, are as ancient as the hills. Why leave a good spot, where you have water, and shelter, and good land?

Constant use, constant change, signatures scribbled over each other... The becks that come down from the high moor in these deep ghylls are fringed by trees, and each almost into living memory had its little mill – or more than one – driving the hammers of fulling mill and the bellows of forge, or the quiet patience of small-grinding millstone. How old? who knows? Below where I stand, a leat once led the water to a pile of stones that was once a hat factory – they made the felt from the local wool, but it was never as good as the true beaver from Hudson's Bay. Across the valley another leat fed the first hydroelectric plant in England. The rent for this manor in the middle ages, payable to the lord of Kendal, was a 'cast of falcons' – that is, a pair of peregrines. Peregrines still do well on the crags above Dent: and gamekeepers, wiser now than once upon a time, let be their stooping. (I used to think it was always deadly, accurate as a well-fired bullet, but apparently they only kill about 10% of the time: they are going so fast they can't cope with a quick jink from a pigeon.) The farm that paid that rent is still there, noisy with sheep in due season and with dogs at all times. Remains of its fortifications are still obvious: the Scots were troublesome visitors along this road south.

A fourteenth century arched door opens to a room with a large TV and armchairs. Forty years away behind it, once upon a time, a steam train chuffed up the slow incline on its way to Kirkby Stephen Lower and then beyond to the coal of Durham. Sometimes I think I hear it.

Look there, deeper into old time: look over the tops of the trees in deep Larum Ghyll, and beyond, on the hillside where the soil was more cultivable to ancient ard ploughs than the heavy land of the valley bottom, there you see outlines of those ancient fields, and a shadow of a ring that once enclosed a Bronze Age barrow. Lower down, you can find the upright stones, rubbed smooth on their edges by generation upon generation of sheep, of a kist burial. Someone has put a metal feeder for the sheep exactly in the rectangle of stone where the body lay. Who was he, or she? Who knows? Except that she was of like passions with us, felt cold, hunger, got ill, had children, died, and was afraid of the dark of that land from which no traveller returned. Like us. And she or he was our relative.

It is autumn now. My autumn too. The boy running around the fields where it was always summer and bringing milk in an enamel can back from the farm down the high-hedged lane to the Vicarage was a long time ago. But I would not have it any other way, for his in-the-moment ignorance did not notice much that was not under his nose. The beeches in the ghylls still are rich in their dull copper leaves. They will spend them in the wild extravagance of the winds that will surely come, when last year's glory will whirl down to form the mould from which new trees will grow. I shall be mould myself one day, like the mould drifted under the hedge I stir with my stick. So be it. Fertile, I hope.

November:

The night is freezing fast,
To-morrow comes December;
And winterfalls of old
Are with me from the past;
And chiefly I remember
How Dick would hate the cold.
Fall, winter, fall; for he,
Prompt hand and headpiece clever,
Has woven a winter robe,
And made of earth and sea
His overcoat for ever,
And wears the turning globe.

A.E. Housman

Winter

Wynter wakeneth al my care,
Nou this leves waxeth bare;
Ofte I sike ant mourne sare
When hit cometh in my thoht
Of this worldes joie, hou hit goth al to noht.
Nou hit is, and nou hit nys,
Al so hit ner nere, ywys;
That moni mon seith, soth hit ys:
Al goth bote Godes wille:
Alle we shule deye, thah us like ylle.
Al that gren me graueth grene,
Nou hit faleweth albydene:
Jesu, help that hit be sene
Ant shild us from helle!
For y not whider y shal, ne hou longe her duelle.

Nobody knows who wrote that sad, fearful, lyric, recorded
in a single manuscript in the British Library.

41

Thomas Hood (d.1845) – a poet now underrated – also hated November:

No sun, no moon!
No morn, no noon,
No dawn, no dusk, no proper time of day.
No warmth, no cheerfulness, no healthful ease,
No comfortable feel in any member
No shade, no shine, no butterflies, no bees,
No fruits, no flowers, no leaves, no birds!
November!

———•———

It is so hard, in this time of plenty, when in the affluent and prodigal West endemic hunger is rare and in midwinter the supermarket can offer the fruits of summer, to imagine what a hard winter might have felt like even a couple of centuries ago. Poverty killed. Even the poorest in our society, and God knows the increasing number of homeless people on our barren, hard town streets have a tough enough time of it, are better fed and warmer clothed than the vast majority of our ancestors. Thomas Gainsborough's 'Cottage Door' paintings, of which five survive, picture a peasant family, all plump and bonny, at the door of their pretty thatched cottage, from the chimney of which smoke from a warming fire rises. The weather is lovely. Indeed, Gainsborough wrote letters (to William Jackson and the architect Sir William Chambers) saying he wished to retire to a country cottage. The idea of idyllic rural retirement idyll was popular in the late XVIIIth century: and it drew the angry scorn of men, like Rev. George Crabbe, who knew what life for the poor was really like:

No, cast by Fortune on a frowning coast,
[Crabbe was vicar of Aldeburgh]
Which can no groves nor happy valleys boast;
Where other cares than those the Muse relates,
And other shepherds dwell with other mates;
By such examples taught, I paint the cot,
As truth will paint it, and as bards will not:
Nor you, ye poor, of lettered scorn complain,
To you the smoothest song is smooth in vain;
O'ercome by labour and bowed down by time,
Feel you the barren flattery of a rhyme?
Can poets soothe you, when you pine for bread,
By winding myrtles round your ruined shed?
Can their light tales your weighty griefs o'erpower,
Or glad with airy mirth the toilsome hour?...
Here joyless roam a wild amphibious race,
With sullen woe displayed in every face;
Who far from civil arts and social fly,
And scowl at strangers with suspicious eye.

There is a record – not untypical – cited in Adrian Tinniswoode's *Life in the English Country Cottage* of what one eighteenth century peasant left when he died. The house was his landlord's; there was no furniture; there were no tools. He possessed a single smock.

When we came to this part of England it was not like that, at all. But there were old people who still revered Lloyd George – 'He gave us a pension' – and before that huge change, old age and poverty were rightly feared. But even my children, who actually grew up here, cannot imagine the signs of the hardship that had so recently been, and had been taken as normal, that made the mindset of men like Seth and Albert. Nothing was wasted: bits of wood, of metal, would 'come in;' pans with holes in them were mended by the itinerant tinker who still called here in the 1960s; bits of leftover food and kitchen scraps fed the hens; clothes that were outgrown were handed down to the next child – I myself always had my older cousin's cast-offs until I was in my teens, and I did not grow up in poverty. Clothes that really were worn out were cut up and made into tatted rugs, and even after that, they still had a use when the Rag and Bone Man collected them for shredding – to make paper, or the yarn known as shoddy. The bones he collected would sent off to be boiled into glue.

When we first knew this house, that first autumn and winter, the first shock was how cold it was. It was not a particularly harsh winter, but we needed the folding screen behind us as we sat and read by the fire of an evening, and were glad of the heavy sweaters my mother had knitted us. A few mornings, the tap was frozen. It rained. The mud from outside was tramped into the rush mats on the brick floors of the house whatever we did, for there was no shelter where we could take off gumboots before coming in. If the wind came from a northern quarter, we could hear it whistling under the slates and through the loft, separated from us by an inch or so of uninsulated lath and plaster.

A bath was not to be taken lightly. Next door, Kate and Albert had no bath, just a galvanised hip bath that hung on a nail in their coal shed. Once a week or so it was placed in front of the rarely lit parlour fire, and filled by kettle after kettle heated on the Rayburn. We never knew hunger, though our diet, like everyone's, was much more restricted, much more tied to the season, than it became later. If you wanted alcohol, you brewed your own beer, or fermented the fruits of the garden and hedgerow in season. Idyllic, you might say, the simple life. Damned hard work. Some children in the village, even in the 1960s, went barefoot in the summer when at home to save wear on expensive leather. There were people in the village who, during the bad years of the 1930s when work was hard to find, had known their children crying from hunger as times got harder at the end of winter, the Hungry Time, when there was nothing to forage, the new vegetables were not yet ready, and meat, unless a poached rabbit or pheasant, was beyond their means – for 'butcher's meat' was a treat most could not afford.

Why am I writing all this down? What drew me into this reverie? I sit here, with the light beginning to die at half past three, writing comfortably in this same house, now insulated, convenient, comfortable, without too many draughts, heated to an extent we find agreeable (even if our town visitors don't). I feel there is a story to be told of, and by, the old folk, the old forgotten ways. We have no guarantee whatsoever that modern affluence, comfort and security will last. The mortgage we have taken out on the planet may be foreclosed, the pattern of world trade is as brittle as glass.

We need to recognise that fragility and be grateful for the gifts we have been vouchsafed, use them well, not take them for granted, and think of what this land has seen of human joy and human suffering. The countryside our televisions show us as clean, tidy, ideal for the picture on a box of chocolates or a jigsaw, is much muckier, much less idyllic, bloodier, much more scribed with human labour and disappointment and hardship and sheer hard unremitting work. We do not wish the old things back, but should honour those who lived them: our family, our ancestors who made our world which we hold in trust for our children. When the mud clings to your boots and the rain hasn't stopped for three days and it has hardly got light, so dour is the sky, then you get an idea of what so many lived through as they yearned for the warming of the year and the first green shoots of spring.

The midwinter days, when the sunset (when the clouds let you see it) across the field is almost at the end of its southward journey, are not the ones that lower the spirits most in winter: those come in January or February. As a species that evolved near the equator, in these higher latitudes we miss the sunlight our bodies need. Mood and vitality drop. We can't hibernate, and by the time the days begin perceptibly to get longer we are drained of vitality, fed up with the sterility of artificial light – well, I am at least. How wise the ancestors were to have the long festival of food and feast, fun and fellowship at this dull time of year! A Christmas before the Reformation, before the work ethic made everyone uncomfortable, lasted twelve whole days of respite from the dragging labour of the land. But that was a long time ago, though fossils of it remained in country life until my youth.

Here we go a wassailing… I remember singing that as a child with not the slightest idea of what it meant. Once upon a time, in many parts, some 12 people went out, each with a mug of cider, and formed a ring round an apple tree, honouring it with the following spell:

Hail to thee, old apple tree!
From every bough
Give us apples enow;
Hatsful, capsful,
Bushel, bushel, sacksful
And our arms full too!

Toast the tree, *'Wes pú hál'*, (in the Old English, 'Be healthy!'), shout 'Huzza!', drink deep, and the coming year will be rich in apples.

One such fossil of old half-forgotten customs round here was Plough Monday, the first Monday after Twelfth Night. In this parish before WW2 the boys used to blacken their faces and visit the better-off houses, and sing

A sifting of Chaff, a bottle of hay,
See the poor crows go carrying away,
Squeak by squeak they wag their tails.
Hoi Nonney! Hi Nonney!

The last phrase was shouted as loud as one could. One farmer, according to old Mr Benstead, whose luxurious white moustaches used to fascinate my very young children, used to come up to each lad, holding a long trap whip, and give him a sixpence, and then, when the last had got his money they all took to their heels as fast as they could with the farmer's whip cracking and his laughter pealing behind them.

The Plough Monday customs, marking when the lengthening days signalled the return to the hard work of the land, were widespread in this plough country, and even in the 1960s old folk could recall how, in their childhood, the gangs from the surrounding villages, with blackened faces and bells on their ankles, and each one with their Molly (a man dressed up as a woman), invaded Cambridge and danced in the Market Square and outside the many pubs. At nightfall they would knock on people's doors and sing

Mump, mump
If you don't give a penny
We'll give you a good thump.

Would there be ASBOs handed out now?

Robert Herrick, who published his *Hesperides* ('Evening Songs') in 1648 with a defiant Crown on its title page as the Civil War moved to its final bloody close, says that on January 12 the ladies had their own work festival: St Distaff's Day, when they were to start spinning, that endless task of all women of whatever age and station before James Hargreaves' invention of the Spinning Jenny: 'Partly work and partly play/ Ye must, on St Distaff's Day.'

'Green Christmas, full churchyard': often true, like many of these old sayings. It is increasingly rare to get a Christmas that isn't green, and the lanes and droves are by this time of year muddy, cut up with deep tractor ruts, not much fun for walking unless you are a dog. Dogs never seem to mind. Sometimes it is hardly necessary to light a fire.

But there was one Boxing Day, a Sunday, after a Christmas Day when we had eaten our goose with the window open, when suddenly the weather turned. The maximum and minimum thermometer outside the window was visibly dropping. Mid afternoon, dry, really cold snow began to fall – not in the end a heavy fall, a couple of inches at most, but in that still air enough to blanket everything into a beauty the more valued for being known to be, most likely, of short duration. It stopped about midnight. In the moonlight the road through the village acquired a new grace, blanketed in an even, luminous, sensuous white that it seemed a sacrilege to sully with steps or wheeltracks. By first light on the next day there had been a little more snow, but it had stopped: but the cold bit harder, and the sky remained sullen, grey. The few children who ventured out for a snowball fight soon came in again, and the snow was too dry for snowballs anyway. Then a mean little south east wind started to niggle at you as you walked, and by lunchtime it was blowing a full gale. The air was full of tiny snowflakes, getting in nostrils and eyes, and the wind was so strong walking became difficult. Then, at nightfall, the lying snow began to move, huge sheets of it blasting across the Fen on the gale, driving off the fields on the higher land, unstopped by any hedge or windbreak. Ditches – those deep ones that were not quite filled up with white that took a month to melt fully – were edged by the lovely curves of snow cornices.

Where the road ran between two higher banks, the snow settled deep, and cars began to have difficulty getting through. And then one failed, and within minutes the snow began to build against it, and nearly cover it, and all the other cars that came to that impasse had to stop too. Some lower slung ones were buried. Our neighbour, bringing home a tractor from the next village but one, got trapped in the growing drift. Folly it was to get out and walk, so as the snow piled up people settled down as best they could in their cars to sit it out. All night. Yet there had been no more snow.

We woke the next morning to a bitter cold, but the low, bright December sun showed a countryside where all the fields had been stripped of snow by the gale, the ploughed clay on the high land turned to a sullen whiteish grey by the frost, and a world of silence except for Michael's pigs squealing their regular annoyance in their sties just along the road. For no car could move.

Obviously, get out and have a look. Everyone had had the same idea. There were parts of the village – the old quarries, for example, or in the lee of the few hedges, some along the road to the next village – where the snow was really deep. The road was glazed. The children and dogs loved it, and then the adults began to let themselves do so too. Clearly, it was folly to try to drive to work, wasn't it? When one man did begin to try, one of the Parish Councillors said to him, 'If you go, we'll all have to go, so had you not better stay at home today?' He did not take a lot of persuasion, for a village can exert quite a lot of pressure.

A happy day. For a start, people checked on neighbours, elderly or living alone, to make sure they were warm and had food. The children began and the heftier adolescents finished a snowball at the top of the hill by the quarries about four feet in diameter. When given its final push it rolled most satisfactorily, growing all the time, down the lane before plunging into the trees at the bottom by the river. People who had not conversed for years smiled holiday smiles at each other. The man who had tried to go to work had an undignified snowball fight with his daughter. And by the time the sun set in a luminous frosty sky, limbs ached with the unaccustomed exercise, the children went sleepily home to tea, and the lights came on in the houses smiling at each other across the frozen road.

In the night it rained heavily. Traffic was dense and slow on driving back to normality. But we had glimpsed another world, and that could never be quite forgotten.

———•———

New Year: and one of those spells of quiet, dry, grey anti-cyclonic weather, with what wind there is coming lazily off the North Sea. It is hard to be affectionate about this sort of weather: day after day when light seems weaker, days upon damp days of mean little draughts, cold enough to get to your bones, but not cold enough to do interesting things like shooting sudden lances of ice across the still puddles on the drove before they freeze over, or decking the twigs in the lace of hoar frost. (If you look at the hoar frost under a lens – being careful not to breathe for a moment – you see that the spicules have the same angular, fractal, relationship and structure as the ice scaffolding on the puddle.) Even the birds seem fed up. My blackbird, the one who is almost tame, sits on the ivy, doing nothing. He looks as bored as I am with the 'Don't *do* that!' calls of the collared doves on the roof. The dank garden merely reminds of things undone and the last brown bunches of ash keys hang motionless on the bare branches. Soil sticks to gumboots in great lumps.

Despite a day of release from work, up well before dawn. Might as well. Bank Holiday after all. Not much I can do in the garden – this can wait, really, and that will take too long for a midwinter day – so, what to do with the day? Perhaps it will be better to get away from this sort of mud and find another sort on the coast, and go for a long walk. For exercise always makes one feel better: so they say.

The drive east is distinguished by nothing. The car's windscreen is filmed with the thin mud thrown up from the damp road by the tyres of other vehicles and the wipers smear it to intermittent clarity. As the land begins to roll a bit and the soil gets sandier you know you are in Britten country, Crabbe country, Sebald country – yes, they knew about this thin land, its winds, its openness to unexpectedness from the east, and the dead lives scribed upon it. When there is a wind you think, sometimes, you can hear ancient voices whispering secrets in the reeds along the dykes. But the reeds are hardly stirring today. Midas' secret is safe.

We park the car and walk eastward over the shingle bank which the tireless tides have stretched along the coast, across the river mouths, forcing the little rivers of this country to turn south, ever south. A sudden eminence as you crest the rise – merely some twenty feet or so – and there is the grey sea, the widowmaker the old poets called it, the whales' road, stretching out greyly smooth into the deeper greyness till you cannot tell where grey sky and grey sea meet. The surface is like smooth lead. Today it lies as peaceful as a cat being luxuriously and sensuously stroked, with just a curling lip repeating a soft deep sigh on the pebbles of the beach: like quiet breathing. But the claws are only velveted: in even a minor gale the shelving beach throws up awesome crashing lines of chaos, foaming grey-brown waves thumping down on shingle and scraping their fingers to grasp the roaring pebbles as the backwash retracts into the critical curve of the next breaker. I love it like that – exhilarating, but how selfish that is! For a great gale is hard for those who follow the sea, and for those who still launch their little boats into the breakers from these beaches to fish for their thin living. Sometimes the tide tops the bank and partially floods the marshy fields where the cattle graze in the deep summer grass. On those days you cannot get away from the noise, which is everywhere – a dull groundbass in your ears, and you smell the salt two miles inland. But today is not like that; quiet, quiet, quiet. A man fishing, his long beachcasting rod propped on a tripod, sits on a little chair, muffled up, and nearly asleep: he half-jumps when I ask him if he has had any luck. 'No mate, calm and East wind. Never any good. But better than being stuck at home with the kids.' I wish him luck, knowing he will have none, and pass on. Feet sink just enough into the shingle to make walking slow, a minor effort. One foot is higher than the other. It will be the other way round on the way back. But perhaps we won't come back this way. A blackbacked gull watches us from the high tide mark. A skein of pinkfeet geese flies along the coast, calling that cry that reminds me of the high northlands where they breed, where I have watched their courtship. They turn inland, their wings suddenly still, at maximum lift, as with the exactness of a corps de ballet in perfect synchronisation they make to land on the marsh to feed. Their calls are still.

———•———

'Dreich': the word Rosanna Petra used as we opened the curtains this late January morning was perfect: the Scots expresses the dourness, the glumness, the greyness of a day that is neither cold nor warm, just dull, still, sitting on your spirits, with even the woodpigeons not bothering to remind each other, 'My *toe* hurts, Betty!'

I chose not to go down the Fen on a doolie day like this for my pre-breakfast walk, and so set off up what they call a hill round here – though to a man brought up in sight of the fells and moorlands up north the word does still seem optimistic. Still, from its 35 foot summit you can see for miles – at least, you can on a clear day – even to the tower of Cambridge University Library, and Addenbrooke's hospital, and Ely Cathedral. But not on a day like this.

Going up the track with the lime and horse chestnut trees on one hand and Michael's new yew hedge (growing nicely now) on the other, it was so hard not once again to grieve for dear Hector the Labrador, who would always choose this start to his busy walk if I gave him the choice. I do miss that tail waving a few paces ahead, and the important look on his face as he chose the place for his first squat. There has not been a lot of rain, but the slight frost is coming out of the marly ground, and where a tractor has run along – Andrew, I guess, going up to see to his portly Dexters – the soil is sticky.

I get into a nice rhythm in the wood, which is ideal for going into deep thought and a sort of half-forgetfulness of one's context. I find that rhythmic, meditative bodily action particularly helpful when I am trying to sort out an intractable problem. I remember one, not that long ago, which preoccupied me almost obsessively for weeks: how to structure the book I was then writing, what to call it, how to focus its themes. My agents, who had handled three books of mine, were not a lot of help: they said they loved the writing but it crossed so many marketing categories they would have difficulty getting a publisher to take it. (I quoted to Bill, who used to handle my stuff, what old Mr Bertram Foyle said to me, then fresh out of University and feeling my oats a bit, the first day I joined his publishing firm: 'Forget all that fine writing, dear boy, just remember that books have to sell, just like frozen peas. Your poor wife can't buy nice clothes on fine writing.' Bill had nodded, sadly.) The book was a travelogue, a memoir of many things, place and people – a pilgrimage of sorts to some sort of acceptance of what we are as humans: both the glorious and the vicious are in each and every one of us. It went from the amphitheatres of Rome to the gulags and the Holocaust – via the glory of Bach, the vision of Dante, the wisdom of Plato, and Gothic arches aspiring to the uncreated light – and the fellowship and friendliness of food shared by a southern sea, and wine pressed on a guest who did not share their language and was born of their ancient enemy, in a little gasthof somewhere near Dachau. (I could, glumly, see what Bill meant.)[1]

Well, someone once gave me very good advice, the more useful in our world which so values instant solutions when actually there are none. John told me to let go, to let the mind play on the problem – any problem: and then let, trust, the subconscious, synthesising, mind to get to work, and you might wake up with the solution one morning, as if magically knowing how to do that awkward bit of bricklaying, or carpentry, or whatever… and if the problem was a bit of writing, spend the next week of waking hours furiously drafting it, oblivious to all except food and drink accepted with a grunt. It has happened before, with one of my books on Shakespeare. But not predictably. Writing is bloody hard work and the rewards can be infinite, but materially infinitesimal.

I stopped to talk to Ron's ram. He is not writing a book. We have been introduced, but I can never remember

---

[1] Well, it was published; *Hungry Heart Roaming: an Odyssey of Sorts* (London: Eyewear Publishing 2021)

his name. He chews thoughtfully, with that sideways motion I can't imitate. (My mother: 'Empty your mouth when you are talking to someone!') He's a friendly sort of beast and likes having his forehead scratched. But he can decide to butt you with that hard head, and as he weighs well over a hundredweight, watch the look in his yellow eye with its horizontal mandorla of black pupil. I suppose it is the nearest thing he can get to being playful. Once he was a charming lamb weighing a few pounds, who butted his fellows off the bales of hay, did not have a huge appendage to encumber his frolics, and who did not have stern duties to perform. But those duties are over now, for this year, and all he has to do is eat his head off. Does he dream? I wonder. Of what?

The first catkins are dangling like lamb's tails from the hazels. The bush at the corner by the very best of last year's blackberry bushes – the old countryfolk called them 'mulberry' bushes – is covered with them. Not a bit of wind stirs their yellow delicacy. And there is another sign of spring in the suddenly sharper green of the lichens on the trees. A chaffinch is trying out its spring song – not very confidently yet. Too early, chum: there is a lot of weather to come. In the shade, where a frozen puddle has drained overnight, a lattice of white ice needles hovers over the dark mud. In the grove by the track going down to the Green snowdrops – I love their French name, *perce-neige* – are out, great patches of them under the bare trees. The green is deserted. But in this still air sound carries. A quarter of a mile away someone slams a door– so it sounds like – and the whole village echoes. (Not Ibsen's Nora, I am sure.) I slip into church, read part of the Book of Amos the Prophet – golly, how up to date he sounds, with his diatribes about the obscene luxury in which live some of the mega-rich, and corrupt business swindling (give it its right name) the poor! And then the next reading for today's Office is some of wise St Paul's humane advice to his beloved Corinthians. Now, with thanks, time for breakfast.

Not so dreich, after all. And I have remembered his name: Sidney.

———•———

January: Marmalade Time, when the bitter Seville oranges appear in the shops and glow on market stalls. My lady makes good marmalade, chunky, not over-sweet, colour an orange deepening to brown. As she puts no additives in it, it does have a tendency when opened to lose its first firmness that you can cut with a knife, and deliquesce, and you have to use a spoon, and it is runny and drippy on the toast. But it is grand.

It's a pretty big operation, and I have to get my own lunch when she is making it: and keep out of the sticky way. For years I kept the big aluminium pan, which holds two gallons, which my parents used for jobs like this, but She has decreed, rightly, that no aluminium will be used when she is cooking. First the cutting and slicing, then the boiling, boiling, boiling until a drop of the seething thick liquid dropped on a cool plate solidifies. Then the ritual of jarring – where I am called in, to hold things for a wife (who has marmalade in her hair from pushing it back with her sticky hand) in a kitchen where most surfaces can surprise with stickiness. The golden stream, with occasional hiccups from the lumps, is smoothly poured into the recently sterilised jars that we have been saving over the last few months. Then we seal it, and hope it was indeed ready to set.

And setting does matter. This yearly rite takes me back to many an early year. My uncle the vicar's country parish had farms and houses far asunder. He did not drive, so his wife took him on his pastoral visits, and when a very young me was staying, I would go with them. (She sang hymns at the top of her not inconsiderable voice as she drove the Morris 8, maroon with black mudguards, through the narrow lanes at speed. Grass grew in the middle. She occasionally met a stray sheep.) At this time of year, when winter is just thinking about one day becoming spring, all the farm and cottage kitchens would be full of the scent of boiling marmalade. I liked those visits, and loved the smell, and the farm dogs I was coming to know quite well, so they only barked at me to show they could, and then wagged, and wiggled, and smiled as only dogs can do. I usually got given a piece of new bread, or a scone, and those never come amiss to a young and always hungry stomach feeling it was a long time since breakfast and a very long time indeed to lunch.

One morning, almost everyone in the parish was in the middle of making marmalade. We had seen the market stalls full of the golden pyramids of oranges in Kendal the previous day. Full jars stood cooling on many tables, and at almost every visit... 'Vicar, do have a pot of my new marmalade. I think you will like this one'... and yet another pot was deposited, upright, among all the others on the leatherette back seat. By the time we turned for home and lunch, there must have been at least a dozen and a half: Seville orange, lemon, orange and lemon, quince ... I sat next to them, and it was when we went round yet another bend in the bumpy lane rather fast that I began to feel a cool stickiness on the bit of my thigh that stuck out of the short trousers that were getting too small. Too true: the jars had fallen sideways, and many, with only paper tops held on by elastic bands, had discharged their contents into a glorious mess all over the back seat, dripping down between the backrest and the seat. I was sitting in a pool of sweetness.

There was a certain consternation, and as soon as we stopped I was sent off to take my trousers and underpants off in the porch and to go upstairs and have a wash. When I came down in a dressing gown my aunt's large bottom was sticking out of the back door of the car and I could hear her singing in a rather subdued voice (she was after all nearly upside down) one of her favourite hymns, 'O God our help in ages past,/ Our hope for years to come' as she spooned up the sticky mess – now a blend of Seville orange/lemon/quince – into jars. For in those years after WW2, when things were still rationed or hard to come by, you did not waste anything, and if the marmalade had in it a bit of muck from the back seat or a twig or two, well, worse things happen at sea. Or, as they say in Lancashire, 'Tha mun eat a peck o' dirt afore tha die.' (Do they still, I wonder?)

She never did get the marmalade that had found its slow way down to below the seat, and for weeks, when it had been shut up and standing in the sun, the car gave off a most interesting odour when you opened the door. As the year warmed, the queen wasps coming out of hibernation – well, they were like wasps round a marmalade pot.

———•●•———

'You can always be sticking in a tree,' an old Westmorland farmer once said to me. Yes: November through to February, when the weather keeps you off the land for any other reason, you can make a promise to the future with a hazel nut, an acorn, a slip, a sapling. I do. It is never too late or too little. I came across, a few days ago, the Chinese proverb, 'What's the right time to plant a tree?' 'Twenty years ago.' 'And the next best?' 'Now, a time which lasts for ever.'

I have planted a lot of trees in my life here. Some, stupidly, I put in the wrong place, and had to cut down, but there are still about 80 whom I set round and about this village and the next. I am particularly pleased with a stand of lime, ash and sycamore which have grown into a respectable spinney. For I have always loved trees, even as a child, without knowing why. From the attic window of my childhood bedroom I could look out to the distant wind-sculpted coverts that dotted the green plain of the Fylde, and long to be there, where I was not allowed to go. I grieved when I saw one of the nearer of those little woods, when in full leaf and humming with summer life, bulldozed and burned to clear the land for a pox of bungalows. My indignant ten-year-old self – even at that age I did indignation rather well – wanted to go and tell the men off.

After all, trees are our fellow creatures, they share the planet with us, and on their exhalations our inhalations depend. We have a common ancestor aeons ago, and about a quarter of our DNA matches that in trees. Our haemoglobin and their chlorophyll have identical structures, save that chlorophyll is built round magnesium while haemoglobin is built round iron. In their rings we read the weather centuries ago, sun and storm, drouth and flood, heat and cold – of what it was like to grow when the world was younger. A forest shares a history, which each tree remembers, records, even after it has been felled. To me, trees have always had different personalities, even within a species. They exhale different scents. They all speak with different voices, from the roar of a big oak resisting, playing with, outshouting a gale, to the whispering chatter of aspen and poplar in the lightest of summer breezes. I understand instinctively why the ancients revered trees, sometimes giving them spirits, dryads.

Who has not been in a wood, alone, quiet, and felt sometimes an antagonism, sometimes a welcome, sometimes almost a Presence? (Silly rhetorical question: *far* too many have not.) I can fully understand the reverence so many civilised Germans – and central Europeans generally – I know seem to feel for the forest. For trees do demand some reverence from us. They have watched out many lives of men, good or bad, and when they die they still serve us, if only to keep us warm. We fill our homes with dead trees: books, shelves, the tables we eat off, the chairs we sit in, and whatever. Once the woods covered Europe, from sea to sea, and the few survivors like the yews of Llangedrnyw in Conwy, or Tisbury, Wiltshire, or the olive of Luras, Sardinia – all over 4,000 years old – recall their ancient dominion – like Tolkien's Ents.

And what I find really exciting is that recent research indicates a secret life of which we had not dreamed: they work not just as individuals but as a mutually supportive community, interacting with each other, supporting the weaker ones, signalling alarms and alerts when under attack from fungi or parasites. They – well, *talk*? – to each other along the nerves of their secret roots, in symbiosis with the mycelia and mycorrhizae that make the very soil a living thing. Sometimes their roots meet, grow together, *merge* in a closer union than any marriage. I am told that the largest trees in forests – the very ones the loggers want to cut down – work as central hubs: some have called them 'mother' trees, with a question-begging but seductive anthropomorphism, for vast subterranean mycorrhizal networks. The mother tree nurtures seedlings by infecting (is inoculating a better term?) them with fungi and supplying them the nutrients they need for growth.

A poet friend of mine once said, 'Trees in their community intercede for us.' Stand in a still, cold, clearing, as I try to do each winter, and shades of an older world, the dark, fierce freedom of trees, press on you. Or on a spring morning sit, or stand, quiet, with your back against an old tree, breathe deep and slow, let its slow life ground your thoughts. Stop. Breathe deep. Listen. Rest your back against this friendly trunk. The trees are rarely quite silent. They move, susurrate. Their talk is slow, never hasty, for they have lots of time in which to say it. The silent tiny stir of pine needles catches on their shine the momentary change of light.

Later in the year, come spring, the sunlight highlights the shrill green of the new beech leaves, which will turn to face the sun as it moves round, and darken with the summer's heat, and ripen into autumn gold. The green male flowers, in twos and threes, hang down on slender stalks, stirred by the flaws of wind that reach this quiet place. The female flowers, bristly little pompoms, discreet, promise nuts and the risk of an unknown future. And then, summer, and the buzz of insects will tell how much the work of life is going on. In the shafts of sunlight, hoverflies. The smooth grey bark of the beech is cool to your back. There are tiny hairs you can hardly see on the surface of the young leaves.

Man is the late comer in this drama. Trees reach back to a world when we were not. High on a Spitsbergen moraine, last summer, I found their tropical leaves in coal laid down in forests when no Man was and that ancient land was half a globe from where it now is scoured by the Arctic winter storms. They wait: they have lots of time. One sign of a sort of hope is if you leave a bit of land, even a building site, untouched for a few years, and scrambling bramble will begin to nurse sycamore and ash, and birch. The waiting trees, left alone, will surely close in wholly when our houses are no more. But our economic (and moral?) blindness continues to demand the permanent loss of what had long been and what might have been, even to the heartbreaking rape of the community of the rainforest by the idiotic selfishness of international capital and politics. They always take back, in their patience, what we took from them for a space and thought our own. They can endure. They have even taken back Chernobyl and greened over the scars of our hubris.

I ought to go out and get away from this desk. My back is getting tired, and the screen is playing merry hell with my eyes. But... I must get on, ignore a wind that all day has trying to attract my attention, ruffling the ivy on the shed and streaming out the slender weeping willow twigs. It's been one of those days, all bright sky and exhilarating wind, that calls you out to enjoy its boisterous, bright energy.

Now the light is going... The wind seems to be dropping, near sunset: I have often noticed that. In the trances of the blast I can hear a cock pheasant proclaiming he is going to his roost. Then another gust makes the climbing rose tap at my window: 'notice me'. There will be a fine sunset over the Fen, and the geese will be calling, and the early tawny owl will be shivering his call to freeze small animals in their tracks. But I must finish this: my sentences are my sentence... the penalty of the temporary joy of netting in words what you are trying to see – and knowing it will always escape. The more I am tempted to down tools and go out, the more conscience pleads unfinished business. But, says the pheasant, and the cock blackbird's alarm in the hedge bottom shouts, 'Listen: we are real. Join us.' I try to ignore that summons to the unexpected and the elemental. But... Do I dare?

———◆———

The elemental: a still, frosty evening. On the coast where I grew up the cold sands and mud flats will stretch far out, for this is the time of the spring tides when the sea withdraws into itself before coming back higher and stronger. There, and here, the geese honk as they fly, dark sounding skeins against the sunset coming in to feed. They constantly shift lead position to spread the burden of breaking trail through the resistance of air. A fox barks, and the sound carries far across the Fen. Muntjac deer, newcomers a few decades back and now claiming the place as their own, bark their harsh monotone cry.

On an evening like this, if you are lucky, you may get a murmuration of starlings – no guarantees, for wild things do not run to timetables or TV schedules. A winter congregation from all over the north, from as far away as Siberia, meets outside our back door. Thousands of little lives come together in one great Beast in the Sky. For sometimes twenty minutes, from when the last limb of the sun drops below the western horizon, the great shape swirls, and swoops like a hunting peregrine, and towers up like a wave breaking against a cliff, and flattens, and finally funnels down like a tornado in reverse into the undergrowth where a scrubby growth of reeds and brambles and little trees fringes the small mere the National Trust has constructed on the part of the Fen the turf-farmer had wrecked. A quotidian mystery, awe-inducing, a perennial puzzle – what is an individual when so many, each flying a unique trajectory, seem simultaneously to think and act as one? 'I am because we are,' as someone once said?

After the first exhilaration, the joy of the rush of speeding wings overhead as the display come to its end with the genie going back into the bottle, a solemn quietness of the mind falls. We rarely speak, for what it there to say about this mystery?

The new moon is setting, thin as a nail paring, in the still luminous west with Venus flaunting her beauty above.

I did give in, as you have gathered, and came back to my desk no wiser, but more grave. And ashamed that my youth never saw such things with these eyes and questions. How could I have missed seeing *that*? What am I missing *this* time?

———•◦———

The two of us had independently thought that it was time we had a day off, and as we went to bed and shut the curtains against the bright stars, agreed that if the weather was good the next day would do as well as any other as neither of us had any engagements. We woke later than usual, which, conscience quiet, itself gave a sense of holiday. It was a sharp, bright, morning, with a hard frost. We decided we would walk down to the washes of the Cam, for when I had driven past at sunset a few days before the water they hold in winter was covered with flocks of migrant waterfowl – pintail, pochard, tufted duck, widgeon, and the geese I love. (I have reservations about the aggressive and invasive Canadas, to be sure, but the pinkfeet and the greylags are always welcome visitors back from the far, far north.) I had stopped the engine, and the quiet sunset was filled with the whistle of widgeon, the indignation of mallard, and the parleying of geese. Worth coming back to listen and see properly, I thought.

My new gumboots are far heavier than the old ones, friends who gave up their soles recently, and I would feel that extra weight after some six miles. But they do have thick Vibram soles, and the ruts on the droveway would be hard to the feet. When we crossed the bridge at the bottom of the lane we could see that our little river, slow at the best of times, was gripped by the ice, even where it is sheltered by trees and steep banks at the bottom of the garden. Where it widens out, by the hythe where decades ago the barges used to unload, the swans had been keeping the water open. When the ice gets thicker, more than cat ice, they clamber up, a picture of ungainliness, onto to the edge and their weight is usually enough to break a substantial sheet free, which then slides under the unbroken ice and freezes there. So you have a pattern of triangles which in low sun is picked out by shadows of the tiny lee of the overlapping plates. This is not a real freeze, of course: I have seen – but it is long ago now – the river frozen for miles, and people skating from village to village.

One winter in particular, soon after we first came here… the entire village was playing on the ice. The air is full of shouts, and laughter and screams of alarm. As you get further from the crowd, the rhythmic sussuration of skates as someone moves fast into solitude along the river resonates in the echoing ice, just as, waiting at a level crossing, you hear the rails sing long before you see the approaching train.

With a sudden emphatic rasp on a turn or a parallel stop, there is tubby Derek: usually surly, now smiling and affable, gliding by on his father's skates, his flat cap still at the usual truculent angle. Old Harold Sennett, as round as he is tall, has become a thing of infinite grace, swooping by bent double, arms behind his back in the old fen fashion, on his long Fen runners, cap back to front – for he goes fast and was a champion speed skater in his youth – over his deep-set black eyes. A swallow among sparrows: for the children are sliding about and getting in everyone's way, including one woman who is nervously using a chair as a Zimmer frame. The younger end, boys and girls together, are showing off to each other with a to-be-noticed hilarity, like the figures in the corners of an Avercamp winter scene. In among all this, romping with excitement, unchecked, cavort three dogs, engaged in unspeakable but all too visible pursuits. The sun goes down over the black fen the colour of the rose hips that still linger on the dog roses in the hedge, and the first star appears. With the sun, the temperature sinks noticeably, but the sound of young laughter echoes for long yet across the frozen fields.

Then there was another, later, winter when my son brought his new Dutch wife – they had met when he was living in Holland – to see us, and they brought their skates. To see them skating along on those long Dutch runners, hand in hand, pace for pace in perfect rhythmic harmony, graceful as the flying geese, was something I shall never forget. And Marian gave me, later, a pair of old *doorloper* skates from Friesland, which too rarely have I used for lack of winters with decent ice, as our poor world warms.

I digress… but it does not matter: I am not writing in my best suit, as it were. The bank stretches straight for miles, bends a little where another lode – that is what they call these canalised rivers of the Fens – joins, and then runs straight again to the lock into the Cam. Being high above the drained fields, you can see for miles, and in this light everything is as sharp as a pin. The winter wheat is reaching its slim fingers up to the sun, the long green lines of the drills ruling the black soil of the fen almost to a vanishing point way across the huge field. Beyond the field, the main drain takes the water to be lifted out of the Fen by the pump down on Cam bank.

On the other side of the river, the National Trust has bought the land for re-wilding. Looking that way, we have the sun at our backs, and seeing is easier. The flashes – not as much water as last year, by a long chalk – are frozen, and hundreds of birds are standing or sitting on the ice. Nearest, greylags, heads under wings, with one old goose sentinel. By the old willow tree that has had its feet in water for years, a few Canadas, and a solitary, smart shelduck. I do hope its mate arrives soon. In the bare branches, two cormorants. But beyond, a huge flock of widgeon, and another of mallard: for the species tend to keep themselves to themselves, not speaking each others' language, almost pointedly ignoring each other.

Suddenly, for no reason I can see, the flock takes off with a clamour of wings, up into the sky in tight array, and wheels round excitedly over the ice as if to set off now, but now, let's be going, early as the year is, back to the north to breed. They will do that in earnest next month. But that little wingstretch over, they lose height once more in a graceful fast curve, and, webbed feet extended, come in to – well, not land, but you know what I mean. Through the glasses I can see several who slightly misjudge, and slide along the smooth ice, bumping into their unimpressed fellows. What secret life do they have?

We walked back along the quiet Fen road, buckled and heaved by the shrinking of the ground – peat is a weak subsoil – and the weight of modern farm traffic. We pass the place where they wash carrots and waste so many because they are not *quite* the right shape or size and 'The Housewife' – a very dodgy concept – will not buy them. Did anybody ask? Or is it one more example of the tyranny of the supermarkets? I once asked a stall selling Fen carrots on Cambridge market if they had any dirty carrots, because they really do keep better. 'Never get asked for them, sir.' 'But I am asking for them?' 'But there's no call for them, sir…' (This could go on for a long time…) Once upon a time I used to go and get a few bucketsful from the heap of waste to feed to our hens and the horse – and of course we had a few ourselves. Perfectly eatable. But because they had been washed they did not keep.

Near the village we meet a runner in a high-vis vest panting along, and on a lead he has a diminutive Chihuahua running like blazes to keep up. It's one way of giving a dog a run, but I am sorry for the dog. Nor did it have a high-vis jacket.

And so home to my beloved's soup and olive sourdough bread. A good morning.

———————•·———————

Jenny and I had grown up in the north west, in the fat Lancashire countryside of the Fylde, that flat plain between the unquiet sea and the first heavings of the hills. I could see those fells in the blue distance from my childhood bedroom window. Trees and rich hedges, and grass, with black and white cattle grazing, and sheep occasionally bought in to fatten, made up our idea of the countryside. This bit of England was at first a shock. Beyond the house, the flatness seemed to reach for ever, beyond the westerly sunset. Few animals, and then after a few years none – for farmers have to respond to the market: all arable. The fields here were ditched, not hedged, and the landscape when we arrived was almost treeless.

Instead of the boisterous and overmastering westerly winter winds of the north-west, we now had mean northeasters in winter. The village called them lazy winds: they could not be bothered to go round, so they went right through you. 'That old wind, he do come straight from the Urinals', said our neighbour Kate that first bitter winter when we felt it for the first time. And true enough, give or take a syllable. On the droveway behind the house, which the tractors hauling sugar beet from the fen had churned up into mud a foot deep, that 'black frost' wind could turn the ruts into iron-hard ridges and furrows that, while the cold lasted, would stand the weight of a cart.

The Fen was never the same. In summer we felt heat and drouth as we never had it at home, where the sea always breathed over the land on even the hottest days. Fine dust rose from footfall and wheel. Horseflies with beautiful green eyes settled silently on exposed flesh. Burdock luxuriated – how did it ever combine with dandelion to make that drink I loved as a child? – and its purple flowers were covered with sipping butterflies. Smells: smells of hot grass, and the rankness of elder. Down the fen, beyond the marly fringe land and onto the black peat, the smells changed. The baking soil smelt slightly sour, newly scoured ditches smelt of water and the cut weeds – a slightly sharp, apple-like, smell – and everywhere, if you worked it, was the staining stickiness of the black fen. For days after you worked it, that soil tanned the lines in your hands. Sometimes in winter the water lay on the fields for weeks, and hungry birds picked at the edges of the pools for the small creatures drowned in the flood. Even a fox could sometimes be seen scavenging where the little waves driven along by the restless wind broke along the little tidemark of twigs and bits of grass and the odd dead thing.

In some winters, a good hard frost as we had never felt at home in Lancashire: and if there were fog as well, every twig, every blade of grass, was fringed with a filigree of frozen lace. Hair became highlighted in rime. You brush it off, and a tiny fall of cold momentarily touches your cheek. There were mornings when as the sun got up you realised that the fog was not very deep, and there was a brightness in the air, and then the weak heat began to penetrate and the lace began to turn to glassy prisms of water, pendulous bursts of light on each twig. Brightness was everywhere.

Fog: you expect fog at this time of year. Just get a high pressure system sitting still, and there you are. Yet there are many sorts, if all the same cause. Fog arrives as soundless as thought, as tender as sleep. First, thin as a chiffon veil, in a hollow of the land, it blurs the trees' stark lines into a drawing half rubbed out. Then a fleece spreads to mask the world in quiet inscrutability. In that deep down, light pales, sounds dull. Droplets glisten on a sweater's wool. The dog's back is wet to the touch. The curve of the path ahead might go to, disappear to, nowhere. Birdsong is silenced, even the jackdaws hold their breath. A drop drips from a leaf to break the stillness.

Sometimes scarves of mist, never very deep, form on the flat land as the heavier cold air flows down from the high land – well, see them from the clear top of the hill and the whole Fen can be swathed in a tissue of white cloud, and you stand on the Sunlit Uplands looking out over a quiet white sea. But then there are other days when it hardly gets properly light, and everything drips, drips, drips a clamminess on every surface. The grey bark of the trunk of our nearby beech is streaked with wet. Even the tops of nearby trees are indistinct. The thick air damps sound, like everything else. Even the monotone chugging of a tractor getting on with ploughing just across the river sounds far away. Cars go past the house, wheels hissing on the wet, mud-slicked tarmac of the lane, slowly, their lights hardly visible. It's tough, a nuisance, if you have to go anywhere, but, in an odd way, beautiful. It goes dark early.

And sometimes the really cold fogs come, when every twig, surface, spider's web is highlighted in white. The edges of the dark green holly leaves are furred with frost crystals, and the tips of the lanceolate leaves of the yew shine white against their collective darkness. The lane is glazed. If the sun does break through, and the temperature goes up just above zero, for a moment or two you can hear the tiny noise of the rime falling. And the world is suddenly bright, the road just now white with rime a sudden wet black ribbon.

As long as it does not go on too long…

———————◆●◆———————

This garden for as long as I have known it is divided between two robins. Obviously, over that length of time they are not the same ones: but it is clear to me that the south-west half is one territory, and the north-east another, and the No Robin's Land runs roughly diagonally across the lawn. Forget about robins being sweet, pretty, red-breasted creatures who show up on Christmas cards or perch companionably on a gardener's spade for a photo opportunity. To be sure, when digging I have had robins looking for food in what I turn up so close to me, so apparently tame, friendly, one might say, that they can be a nuisance. It is so easy sentimentally to think they trust you, like you, are somehow grateful to you. But not a bit of it: they are out for the main chance of an easy meal. They are also among the most belligerent and bad-tempered of the small passerines.

A striking demonstration of this happened this morning. I was sitting with a cup of coffee after doing some tidying in the vegetable patch, which is in the north-east half of the garden, during which a robin had been intermittently with me. As I sat on a bench in the south-west half, a robin flew from behind me over the DMZ towards the veg. No sooner had he landed – I know it was he, as he had the whiteish throat of the male – than out of the north-east bushes came a second male, at speed. The two immediately sang loudly and then set to. And they meant it. Unlike so many birds where there is a lot of displaying and threatening until one backs off with no physical contact, these two went at it hammer and tongs on the lawn for a good few minutes, pinning each other down, pecking at each other, flying up breast to breast with their little claws – big to other robins, and sharp – reaching out to scratch at each other. They rolled over and over, and gradually the bundle of fury got into the DMZ. Whereupon they separated. One – I suspect the defender – flew up into the nearby apple tree and sang deafeningly, while the defeated one crouched on the ground. The singer then flew off, back into the bushes. The first robin sat there, then seemed to catch sight of me – I was only seven or eight yards from him – and appeared to pull himself together. He almost shrugged. 'Huh, I wasn't really scared, you know. I let him have his little triumph. One does from time to time.' He preened and put his disordered feathers in order, and then – I swear it – looked me in the eye with his left eye, flew up onto a branch above me into Antonia's Birch, and sang his Lilliputian heart out as if he were the victor. Saving his face. Comedy, yes. But thought-provoking.

———————•———————

This year has been a good year for moorhens. The shaggy overhang of brambles and other bushes on the steep banks of the river at the bottom of the garden usually holds two or three nesting pairs. Too often, however, their hatched balls of black fluff, scuttering like blown down across the surface, get drastically gobbled by an indolent pike who sits in a deep swanhole near where the brambles arch over the river to give the nest shelter. He (she?) wasn't there this year – and a ghost of a worry stirs my mind, like a flaw of wind on water, for there seem to be far fewer fish in the river than there were even a few years back. So our Mrs brought off and raised five young. They stayed together through leggy, dun, youth, and right to their mature plumage this autumn.

As the windfalls from the apple trees grew thicker on the lawn we saw them more and more often coming up the grass from the water for their breakfast, and dinner, and tea. Of course, apples that are ripe and rotting get to have a significant amount of alcohol – you can smell it – and we did wonder what Mummy was letting her teenagers get up to and whether they were getting hooked. Certainly they seemed to steer a more leisurely, circuitous course back to the river after a good gorge. Such became their passion for apples that sometimes they did not wait for them to fall, but perched on their long legs in the branches to peck at the fruit – very unsteadily, with much keeping of balance with wings and tail.

As winter drew on and time got harder for wild creatures, when some of the apples we had stored went bad, we threw them out – with the cores we ourselves left – onto the lawn for the Gang, as we came to call them. They seemed a companionable bunch, co-operative even, and it became more and more difficult at a distance to tell Mummy apart from the rest as their plumage matured. But today one of the Gang has gone rogue... He (I think it must be a he) is on his own, right up near the back door by the shed we call the Molery (where we store fruit and vegetables, and has just managed with great difficulty to pick up a apple I threw out. He had eaten most of it, but the chunk left is twice as big as his head. He is, well, *staggering* down the garden with it. Have you ever seen *gallinula chloropus* stagger? He did. He got as far as the middle of the lawn and has put it down for a rest and a quick snack. Oops! Mummy has arrived, running with a flap of wings, and told him off in no uncertain terms. He's left the apple and watches while she is tucking in... The elderly have their pleasures too.

———•———

February brings a little lightening of the dark mornings, and a perceptible lengthening of the afternoon. In this part of the world it can be the coldest and toughest month of the winter.

'If at Candlemas you see the sun,
Winter's worst is yet to come'.

The rhyme from Lancashire childhood once – not long ago – had me hopefully looking for the sun on February 2, for I love extremes of weather, the quiet drama and disguise of snow, the mastering energy of storm, and later the hot still quietness of an August cornfield. 'All things spare, original, strange…' Now I bother less, I suppose, for there has been little time to play in the snow in recent years, and other cares have mastered me. (And I am also aware that the old rhyme probably refers to the old calendar, January 22.) But I can recall great freezes in Reach, one in particular in the early 1980s. For most of the winter there had been a run of mild, damp weather, and the roads grew deep in the soft mud that the tractors brought up from the Fen as they hauled loads of sugar beet, an unlovely crop, to the road ready for sending off to the sugar beet factory at Ely. Then the wind went round to the northeast, and stayed there. Old Kate next door years before had explained that that northeaster came those mountains she memorably misnamed in Russia…

Wherever it came from, that black frost wind, blowing its steady ten miles an hour off the European High, turned the wormcasts on the lawn into iron whorls that one could pick up. The wind kept open the river, and the pit where once the gault clay for the river banks had been dug, with wavelets fretting at the stands of winter-brown reeds.

One morning, each reed had at its base a crystal ruff of frozen foam. The ruts of the droves froze hard enough to bear the weight of a trailer loaded with beet. By next morning, the river was frozen, uneven, dissected by straight ribs of ice where the frost finally mastered the wind that had nearly kept the water open. And all the while that wind, and a landscape grey, huddled against it, no rime, no hoar, no snow, just the black frozen earth and the grass grey with cold.

It endured, hardened in. Reach Lode – and the other lodes, though not quite the Cam – froze for a fortnight, and the red disk of the setting sun shone level across the (in the end) snow-dusted fields to catch familiar neighbours (about whom one might usually have reservations), skating along that waterway, elevated above the shrunken peat of the fen, now transfigured into things 'orient, immortal, Cherubims, and yong Men Glittering and Sparkling Angels and Maids Seraphick Pieces of Life and Beauty'! It lasted for more than a moment, that Epiphany, before the light went, and the memory of the village as an Avercamp winter scene has enriched all milder winters since.

Why do people like me so often translate the reality into remembered art so that we can see what we saw? And is it not a wonderful thing that now, with Google Images, we can refer to a piece of art and know that one of your readers can look it up from, as the adverts for Correspondence Colleges and self-medication used to say, the comfort of your own home.

———●●———

Frost was An Event on the Lancashire coast of my childhood. The sea's proximity most of the time kept it away, and autumn and winter were lots of wind and lots of rain and the roaring of the grey sea on that flat beach that stretched for miles when the tide went out. Of course, we did get occasional cold snaps, and I would wake up to the delicate ferns of frost on the inside of my bedroom window. In them my finger nail could scratch patterns, until my clumsy ones had quite over-written the lovely ones I wanted to keep for ever. But by late morning the frost would usually have gone.

Cambridgeshire was quite a different matter, and I can remember frosts that dug deep into the soil and stayed for weeks. Soon after Jenny, my first wife, died, we had the coldest winter snap for decades. It did not last very long, but for a time even this dry countryside, where rain is rare and snow rarer, was blanketed in white and the mercury was going down to -10 regularly. At minus five my beard begins to ice up if there is any sort of wind chill. At minus ten the luxuriating eyebrows of late middle age get an edging of whiter white. And it is the sort of weather that, if I can get out in it, I love. So when out with the dog, whose first experience of snow this was, his blackness and my greying were highlighted in the purest of whites.

The washes beside the Cam, the summer grazing that floods in winter, were frozen to the horizon. Bare willows, old pollards, stood stark out of the ice, marking in some cases the winding line of the old channel of the river before They straightened it. The sheet of ice had been largely swept clear of the dry snow by the wind, and its dull grey sheen was smooth, inviting. Anyone who could take the time hastened through the snow, driving along the narrow icy lanes across the white flatness of the fen, to take advantage of the best skating for years.

Some new to this delight teetered on uncertain skates, the curve of the figure skate's blade not helping their balance, or their confidence, at all. Some few had long flat-bladed Fen runners, which demand a different technique and are ideal for going a long way at speed: I have talked to men and women who, in the great winter of 1962-3, when we ourselves were uselessly stuck in a flat in Cambridge, skated the 18 miles from Cambridge to Ely and back regularly, with time for a drink at the Cutter Inn down where the docks used to be in Ely. One spoke with nostalgic longing of the time he and the woman who became his wife stayed a bit longer than they had planned in the warmth of the Cutter Inn, and skated back upstream hand in hand as the last flush of the sunset sank in the west and the full moon of February climbed above the flat horizon in the north east. A long time ago… But we are made of our memories.

Anyway: back to that brief sharp spell before the high pressure system slipped away and the Atlantic depressions of early spring brought wind and rain, hard ground became mud, and a different sort of insecurity of footfall. I taught my grandson to skate on the Wash, stuffing my boots, far too big for him, with socks and newspaper. He was a natural, but then he had less far to fall. (Later, I taught him to ski *langlauf*.) A joy. The dog slipped and slithered on the unfamiliar surface, puzzled, all four legs rigid, slightly splayed, and then in the end seeming to enjoy it.

And another joy: every day, the dog and I, at first light, and again just before sunset, would leave the house, me carrying my long Norwegian skis, to the little rise we call the hill. Where acres of its top have been quarried away over the last thousand years or so for building stone, for Cambridge, for Ely, for so many humble (and not so humble) houses and barns and granaries and so on, the new wood is just growing to the promise of maturity. Each branch was highlighted in white. The tussocks of grass in the open patches were little mounds of white with, on the downwind side, a glimpse of the dark dead grass within. Beech and ash, yew and holly, hazel and hawthorn, spindle tree and gean – how snow makes you see every time, as if for the first, the different beauties of their nakedness!

The hill does not offer *langlauf* skiing comparable to other places where I have heard the creak of the snow under my runners and the regular swish of my poles: the vast silence of midwinter Norway or the woodland of a special valley in the Dolomites. But it is much, much better than nothing. (And that sort of skiing is wonderful exercise: you feel you have *done* something, and soon get up a sweat.) The sinuous paths through the bare trees take you in the end to the barer top of the hill, whence on a clear day you can see the tower of the University Library in Cambridge – and be grateful you are here.

Then, a long easy slope across the big field where I used to find Neolithic flints, where one can pick up a bit of real speed, down to the drove running along the fen edge – the old road between the villages, before the Enclosure Commissioners built the new one. Hector followed me with excitement as I sped down the hill – 'Pack Leader doesn't *ever* go this fast!' – and romped round me as I stopped. He came happily up the hill again with me, and down again, and up again, and down again… by this time my tracks were getting nicely polished, and the skis were running beautifully, and he could not keep up. Then I got to the bottom, again, and no Hector. He had given up, and was standing on the top of the hill – too cold to sit down.

He had decided it was time to go home. When I got back up to him, his eyebrows were white, his muzzle was white with his breath, and frost highlighted the spare lines of his black body. I stopped, and steam rose from me as from a horse that has been working hard. A good memory, and a good fire of bog oak to warm my back at home.

———•—•———

I said I loved extremes of weather – like storms. It seems very selfish, to be honest, for I know perfectly well how much trouble, pain and loss they can cause to people, and I would not like to share it. But my delight in the overwhelming energy of a big wind is pointed up, I think, by just that little salting of, well, fear. It's so much bigger then we are... It's rather like the exhilaration of tackling a slope on your skis that you are not *quite* sure you really can manage, or the adrenalin rush of a tricky bit of scrambling on the hills. You know you will do it, but you just might not. So a gale roaring in the big willow at the end of the garden, actually bending its strength, actually making the ground under it move as I stand on its roots, so that in the remissions of the pressure it flexes back – I know the wind might bring it down, crushing the first shed I ever built (where all sorts of important and necessary things are kept, and never used), but my guess is it won't. I hope.

———•—•———

By late winter you can usually be sure that the washes by the river – that huge expanse of summer grazing between the raised levees that hold back the winter floods – will be covered in water. The few willows will be standing in the water, a curve of a few old pollards marking where once of old, the river ran. The sheet of shallow water is big enough to have a long fetch, and a steady gale will raise a respectable chop, even miniature breakers. In such weather, spotting the wintering visitors is harder for me than it used to be, with older eyes watering in the blast, and I admire those muffled-up people with huge insulated optics who can sit for hours gazing at what to me are simply distant blobs.

Once a young me used to fish off the beach at Rossall with my feet in the edge of the water, just where the wave exhausted itself before roaring back over the pebbles before the next breaker's curl. Then I could outstare a big westerly and the roar of it, warmed by the hunter's hot lust, my eyes alert for that tell-tale dip of the rod that does not synchronise with the pull of the backwash. But now I have to be satisfied with looking at the miniature tidemark near me, along which, if you are very still and quiet, you will see small creatures foraging. I love best those still, cold, clear evenings when the flooded wash mirrors the cold sunset sky and its shy stars, and the haunting whistle of a teal breaks the silence.

Spring

The first mild day in March. The northern wind has gone west and there feels to be some heat in the sunlight on your back. Sailing up on the breeze come big clouds like buxom cauliflowers – it seems the right metaphor for a gardener to use, though in my own garden I could never manage the frothing glory of that vegetable which old George my neighbour achieved, perhaps by digging his toilet bucket into the soil each morning.

The brilliance of the morning, the green of the young barley lapping at the light, is suddenly dimmed as the shadow of the cloud passes, as if drawing a brush of darker wash over the landscape. But the hard edge of the shadow passes, and the sun is suddenly warm again as you bend to the rhythm of the spade. Bird song is incessant, each minute sweeter than before. Is it fanciful to feel a blessing in the air, which seems to yield a sense of joy to the bare trees? First signs of spring: buds burst with life.

Can trees feel joy?

To March:

A light exists in spring
Not present on the Year
At any other period –
When March is scarcely here
A Color stands abroad
On Solitary Fields
That Science cannot overtake,
But Human Nature feels.
It waits upon the Lawn,
It shows the furthest Tree
Upon the furthest Slope you know;
It almost speaks to you.
Then as Horizons step
Or Noons report away
Without the Formula of sound
It passes, and we stay –
A quality of loss
Affecting our Content,
As Trade had suddenly encroached
Upon a Sacrament.

Emily Dickinson

I feel at this time of year as if I want to be everywhere
I love all at once: way in the west, in this clear light, on
Pilling Marsh, sea-washed grass sheep-nibbled to velvet,
dissected by the dendritic creeks, ever smaller and smaller
as they get further from the muddy shore, between shiny
wet shoulders of boulder clay; Crosscrake with the wild

gooseberries in the hedges just coming into shy bloom by the Vicarage; Rossall with the rollers of the spring tide booming on the miles of flat beach; Middleton as the buds burst into leaf in the coverts and the deer rub the velvet off their antlers in the woods – and our pheasants strut in their glamorous male pride and cry their raucous challenge to all who might presume to approach their dowdy harem. In First Court of my beloved College, just before Evensong, with the clock chiming the quarter and the last of the light aslant on the ancient turf. Or just here, where I am, with the triangular ash buds greening from winter black and their flower tassels just breaking out. Surprised by joy, indeed.

———◦———

This morning, a big wind. Going down the Fen and coming to black fields where seeds had just been set, little wisps of fine soil – dust, really – were beginning to lift and swirl, just a few inches off the ground. It doesn't happen now, not as much. March years ago used to bring them regularly, those Fen Blows. They were serious.

When we first knew the Fens, people were still getting grants to grub out the few hedges left, they were still making the fields bigger and bigger to accommodate the gigantic new machinery – it has got still bigger since – and the place was drained, drained, drained. Old habits die hard: water was the enemy. In spring the fine black peat soil would be set with the new crop, and sometimes on a warm, dry day you could see a cloud of fine dust rising behind the seed drill. But spring is a fickle time. You can get lots of rain – there is always too much or not enough, as any gardener or farmer will tell you – or you can get none. If the former, the land can soon be too wet to get on with heavy machinery, which can easily sink in up to its axles. If the latter...

All you need is the strengthening sun of March or early April, a recently set field, and the top inch of blackness so soon heats up and dries out. Now throw in a big March wind, the sort that often comes around the equinox, and before you know where you are there is a thin blizzard of skin-pricking black soil coursing across the field, a few inches deep, drifts at the ditches and road verges, and if the wind is really big and turbulent, the cloud of dust can rise many feet into the air.

I have stood on a hill looking out over the Fen on a day of gale and seen huge dark clouds sweeping across the Fen, sometimes taking the seed with them. I have tried to drive across the Fen in a Fen Blow, and given up, for it was worse than a blizzard. Cars and tractors battle through its gusting noise with headlights on. I have seen snowploughs out to clear the roads of the black drifts. I have seen ditches with beautiful cornices of black half closing them, like snow smoothly pendulous over a rock face high on a mountainside. I have seen fine black dust behind the wallpaper, coating the windowsills and furniture, even behind the glass of pictures in houses in the path of the blow. Blows were dreaded. For the man in a small way who lost his seeds, they could spell a year that might be ruin.

The suddenly longer evenings after the clocks go forward, and the exponential extending of the hours of daylight, are always for me as if a cork has been taken out of a bottle. For much as I love the sights and sounds of winter, look forward to the arrival of the birds who come from the far North I love, and winter's real pleasures, as I have aged I have found the dwindling of the light harder and harder. We evolved where days and nights were more equal, we can't hibernate, and so there are bound to be consequences bodily and mental in living beyond our natural biological range. Be that as it may: I get fed up by February, and scratchy, and don't make things easier for other people who are scratchy and fed up. And then the clocks change, we curse the lost hour of sleep – and then suddenly one comes home in the light.

By late March, an evening walk is on the cards. After all the rains and storms of February, this March has been quiet as a mouse, and though there have been a few night frosts, the days have warmed to balminess. This evening there is no chance of frost: it is the first shirtsleeve walk of the year. We wander down the drove to the field where Michael has put his cows. A notice on the gate says 'Caution cows with claves [*sic*] and bull.' Fair warning: and one should always be careful not to get between a cow and her young calf. But these are pretty peaceable animals, and the old Hereford bull with the gnarled feet is a quiet fellow whose main delight in life seems to be eating. He is standing by the gate, for all the world like an old gentleman leaning over his garden gate to talk to anyone who passes by on this quiet and lovely evening. I like the old boy, and lean over and scratch his ears. He likes that, and lifts his head so that I can do the other side properly. There is something very – well, calming about massaging a friendly animal's ears, and their obvious pleasure in it. Hector the Labrador used to like it too.

Other people have had the same delight in the evening as we. We meet Thomasina, whose allotment is an absolute picture of well-managed tidiness, with her elderly pointer bitch, and I give her its expected biscuit, and we chat, not really saying anything much (except how good her allotment looks), just enjoying being out and sociable, and feeling at a sort of peace in this golden light. 'Have you seen the hares boxing?' she says, and following her advice we strike off into the flat fields where the wheat is already a few inches high. The man who has this land shoots, and he has left a wide strip of unploughed, unsprayed land round his fields as a place for the partridges to breed and forage. And many other creatures too find it a haven: insects, early butterflies, a glimpsed stoat, and the rough grass is crisscrossed with worn pathways where animals go about their secret business. There is a patch of flattened grass, which is a hare's form: they have several. You can see the deer slot leading to the deep ditch, the deeper prints where the beast took off as it leapt the obstacle. You can see (and smell) where a fox has been doing its rounds, where it went down the bank and up the other side. In one of the angles of the field I think there is a skylark's nest, hidden in the longer grass. Without the shooting each autumn, there would be no point in leaving this untended for all this extra joyous life.

But we are looking for hares. Suddenly, just ahead of us and upwind, the tall old grass by the ditch parts, and there is Puss, sitting up and taking notice. We freeze. The hare has not noticed us, has not winded us, and unconcernedly nibbles a bit of new grass, and lollops off onto the open field. We follow it with our eyes, and see where it is going. Somehow, it must have had a notice of the forthcoming meeting, for way out in the middle of the field are four more, clearly in some sort of occasionally energetic conversation. It's only at this time of year these usually solitary animals decide they need company. The hares, five now, sit some way apart, perhaps having a sustaining nibble of the wheat. But then, suddenly, something disturbs them, and they are off in all directions. They stop, after a sprint of a hundred yards or so, and sitting up, look back. Then off again, off to other fields and pastures new. It was a couple of walkers way over on the other side of the field, upwind, who had disturbed them. We stir, feeling our walk has been worthwhile already, and we can soon turn for home. But evening is a time when other creatures expatiate – lovely old fashioned word! – and take the air, and to our delight the roe deer make their appearance – two groups, a four, and a three – a three? There ought to be two fours. I have seen them before, and they seem to be civil enough to each other, but not on what one might call intimate terms. They stop in their gracefulness and watch us, as we walk past about a hundred yards off. Their big ears are pricked, to catch every sound. They pronk off a few dozen yards, and stop again, for like hares they are full of both timidity and curiosity. We are grateful.

But why only three? We found out why as we walked back a different way. There is a scrubby little thicket in the middle of nowhere where the deer sometimes lie up, and few yards from it, up against the wire fence, is a dead roebuck. His dished back and the sloping coronet at the base of his horns suggest he was past his prime, but this year's velvet is still hanging off his horns. His eyes have been pecked out by the crows, and he has been dead long enough for his belly to have swelled. The flies, the clean-up squad, are moving in. How did he die? I did not check to see whether it had been a badly placed rifle shot, for we do sometimes get clowns from the towns driving out and with little skill poaching the deer – madness, to use a rifle from a car in this flat countryside, for the bullet can go a mile and still do harm to man and beast. But death is as much part of the countryside as are decorous deer and happy hares on a March evening when all seems peace and goodwill.

At least, now, we don't get the gangs of hare coursers as much as we used to, betting on their greyhounds running down the desperate hares. They care neither about their dogs, which are treated on the whole pretty badly, or their quarry: the dead animal, enough meat and more for a family, as I well know, is left to rot. It's the money, stupid: £30,000 can be bet on a single course. And the men who do this are abusive, and threatening. There are always clouds.

But it was a good walk.

———————•———————

I walked alone along the river from Ely to Cambridge. It does not matter why, now. All the way, the river seemed to be full of great crested grebes. I love seeing them, and admire their elaborate surprised-looking heads that seem to be wearing a prick-eared helmet of feathers. I do wonder, though, what evolutionary advantage that gives them when they are chasing their prey underwater. It seems also to have nothing to do with display or sexual dimorphism, as with almost all other species which employ shape and colouration, and it seems almost impossible to tell the sexes apart. (Over my lifetime, that has got to be much more of a problem, not just with grebes.) The grebes can, one hopes: and I find a certain magic in seeing their strange courting ritual when each, breast to breast, presents the other with a scrap of weed. She/he is cheap to keep... would my Beloved like some weed? (No, not *that* sort of weed...) There was a nest in the reeds by where once stood the Fish and Duck pub, much patronised by bargees in the old days when the river was busy with no-nonsense commercial traffic. I caught a glimpse of the nest, and either Mummy or Daddy was on it with either Mummy or Daddy patrolling the river – both sexes incubate, making things yet more complicated. The world is charged with wonder, with the glory of God. Everywhere is a theophany.

———•●•———

I have never depended for my livelihood on the land, but I have been close enough to it to understand those who do. I have haggled with the corn merchant over the price of my ton and a half of barley (and got a very good price indeed, for it was malting quality). I have cut my load of hay, and brought it home with the children sitting atop the load on the trailer in the best of all beds. (Health and Safety would have a fit!) I have known what it is to watch the sky when dashing back from work on the day we had arranged to have someone bale the hay, nervous in case it rained on its sweet-smelling windrows we had laboured to make (work that is hard on the back and arms) in the preceding days. I know how back-breaking, and sapping, and lonely, work on the land can be, and I do not romanticise it. But my peasant soul is still warmed each year by the first broad beans thrusting their green fists up through the soil, and unclenching them to grasp the light and air, by the yearly thrill of the first potato leaves to appear.

We have finished the frozen broad beans and dwarf beans. A thin, even hungry, time of year this was for many poor folk, until a single lifetime ago. People ate ground elder as a salad; and for afters, rhubarb to 'clear your blood.' My late leeks, that have overwintered, are suddenly putting on girth, and spreading rich dark green leaves to the returning sun. If we don't soon eat them all up, we shall start to find at their heart the hard uneatable stem of the flower shoot. Some always do get away, and I always try to let a few flower, for the bumble bees love those tight balls of florets. Some people ask me for them for dried flower arrangements… Then the asparagus: fresh pale green spears impaling the sunlight. It is the first vegetable of the new year. I am awfully proud of them. For on a visit with friends to Tuscany they insisted on going to a garden centre – a waste of good church-crawling time – and while they were there I browsed the seed packets and came up with these. And every time I eat them I think of Lucca, and Boccherini and Puccini, who were born there. The stored spuds from last year are soft and hairy with chits. Some I shall plant: once growns often do well.

A fine weekend, and those who garden or have allotments are hard at it, getting a tilth on the land, planting seeds, setting potatoes. It's a cheerful world.

Men pass and talk about, well, the weather. 'Grand day, but we could do with some nice warm rain. Land needs a good soak.' – and infinite variations on that, and on offers of spare seeds or onion sets, or recommendations of varieties. What we are all really saying is, 'It's spring! I am so enjoying this, aren't you?'

———•———

The year 2020: this spring will always be remembered as the Coronavirus spring, and as I write this the final outcome is still wholly unknown and beyond guessing, whatever temporarily powerful politicians say. But what is certain, and obvious, is that like all things this pandemic will come to an end. Nevertheless, in the regular cycle of the turning year, seedtime and harvest, so immemorial, suddenly everything seems emotionally adrift, in question. Including, to be blunt, one's own survival. Will I ever finish this book? (I hope I live to see that question in print…) But like wise Lady Julian, writing nearly 700 years ago in her anchorhold in Norwich while inexplicable bubonic plague regularly came out of nowhere and killed people in as little as 24 hours, we can say, 'all shall be well, all shall be well, all manner of thing shall be well.' But perhaps not in the way each of us expects, or hopes, for good or ill.

There have been pandemics before, several times. We Europeans started one ourselves when we first went to the New World. The peoples who did not know they lived in a New World were easy meat for Old World microbes. Within a generation some 90% of Native American had been wiped out by things like measles and the common cold. (Their return gift to the Old World was a new, virulent form of syphilis, the only disease I know named after the hero of an epic poem – Girolamo Fracastoro's *Siphilus, sive Morbus Gallicus*, 1530). I have lectured a good deal, over the years, on the world crisis – a dramatic climate shift and a not unrelated pandemic – of the fourteenth century, and it's more fun than any disaster movie. One point I always stress is that almost everything modern society takes for granted – labour-saving machines, the concentration of capital, the market value of labour, a money rather than a customary economy, lay education and literacy, the demise of legal serfdom, and even double entry bookkeeping – came out of people having to respond imaginatively and practically to the initial collapse of the population by around 50% in a single winter.

But, then, nobody knew the rules for the new game, any more than they do now. We are not now in another 1348, or the almost forgotten but almost equally deadly 'Justinianic' plague and crisis of 541, or even 1918, bad enough in all conscience. This virus is not the 'Destroying Angel' of pestilence that the 1559 and 1662 Book of Common Prayer implores God to make to 'cease from punishing.' But the big difference between those thens and now is how intricately connected and interdependent at every level is our worldwide culture. How innocently we trust in science and technology to provide a quick fix! But it can't undo the moving of the intellectual, emotional and imaginative goalposts. Nobody for a long time will be able to relax into an assumption that normal is normal. If ever you needed a demonstration of the Butterfly Effect, here it is: a poorly bat in China is in a cage on top of a pangolin in a market, and a few weeks later the stable world as we know it is brought to a halt, and even American Presidents have to acknowledge that there are some things walls won't keep out. But though it is not yet the Last Trump, there will be changes.

There are already. Nobody is going to work if they can help it, on government instructions. Jobs and businesses have collapsed, at least temporarily. Gardens, after a few days of undivided attention, are almost painfully tidy. Vegetable plots are immaculate, waiting for a nice gentle warm rain to arrive and really get things going. Today was a wonderful bright spring morning, again, after a run of the same, and my beloved and I walked out early while there was still frost in the shade. As we walked seriously along the drove, two yaffles laughed at us in their looping flight – well, not really, but it is nice to anthropomorphise. A solitary heron stood as if thoughtful in the middle of the meadow, and then took off with the slow flap of his huge broad wings. The scent of the opening leaves of the poplars on the river bank came on the wind – a spring smell I find intoxicating, evocative, recalling the scent of the sticky propolis on the bees' frames when I happily used to work their summer hives, cutting through that strong glue to extract the waxen combs and their dripping hoard of sweetness. By the corner of the field that used to be Seth's, where the water of a higher ditch trickles into the lower one with a sound, like a tap left half on, that you do not associate with this flat country, his greengage tree seems to be wanting to start blooming.

I remember when I first came to that spot. We had just arrived in the village, and to help out an elderly neighbour, I drove him down to his field in the Morris Traveller, a cloud of summer dust rising behind us. He wanted help lifting and bringing in his spuds, and never shall I forget the fork going into that black earth and the largest potatoes I had ever seen erupting whitely from its richness. Happy time, and the greengages he gave me were a revelatory delight for one who came from a county where greengages were simply not grown. That was in the days before you could get anything from anywhere at any time... can it last?

Quite a few people are already out and about, taking their permitted exercise. Everyone is trying to be as friendly as possible and as is compatible with keeping an antisocial distance. The village is full of people wanting to be co-operative, helpful to each other. They greet each other with gestures, talk with the river between them, cheerfully exchange news of gloom and uncertainty on a smiling morn when the birds are noisily marking territory and the first hatched pigeon eggshells lie whitely on the grass. Further along the hedge, a flamboyance of magpies takes off from the ground as they see us. What mischief to small birds have they been doing, I wonder? Dogs of course know nothing of 'social distancing', and run up to me as they usually do and get their usual half-biscuit – I always have a few in my pocket. There are much worse places than this spot of England to be stuck in.

Mornings like these, it is hard to keep the sense of seriousness and gloom properly due to what the news on the radio constantly tells of the worsening statistics, the hardship and suffering of others, of whole countries in what is inelegantly called 'lockdown.' The word seems to have originated in southern California in the 1970s, and was used originally of confining prisoners to their cells 'for their own good.' (An ominous etymology...) However... the two of us walked on, further down the Fen and over the new bridge, and into the new wetlands near Wicken – so far they are only teenage wetlands, so to speak, and there is a lot of longterm wetting to do before they develop anything like a true wet fen vegetation. Even so, there is a wide expanse of water, a foot or so deep, ideal for the flocks of russet-headed pochard, a few shelduck, some Canada geese, a few greylags, and the usual indignant coots. On that lone willow tree bleakly in the middle, its feet in water, two cormorants (*can* they be the same ones of a month or two ago?) perch, their black wings half open to dry out. (They have no oil gland above the tail to waterproof their feathers, as other waterfowl do.) The wintering geese, pinkfeet and brent, have been gone north for some weeks now, leaving the washes of the Cam quiet. As we walk past, the longhorned Highland cattle, introduced a few years back as they can thrive on this poor pasture, sit and chew their cud slowly, following us with their longlashed eyes.

We walk on, tacitly agreeing it is too good a morning to waste, and work can wait an hour or so. We pass where the derelict farm buildings were, a tired mess of badly laid brick and rusty corrugated iron, and concrete floors heaved and cracked with the movement of the peat beneath. A pair of barn owls always nested there. I see that someone has set an owl box on the top of half a telegraph pole. It's an ugly enough thing, but I do hope it is Des. Res. for the owls as there is precious little elsewhere where they could go. I have a good look to see if I can see owl pellets, but I can't be sure: after the wind and rain a few weeks back, they could easily be washed out or away. But I have seen an owl hunting silently over this fen this winter. So we may be lucky.

All this fen 'went back' to wet wilderness in the farming depression of the 1930s, and James Wentworth

Day celebrated its wildlife and its wildfowling in his books, and the much-loved local doctor – they named part of the next village Ennion's Corner after where he used to live – spent perhaps more time doing exquisite paintings of the wild birds and writing a lyrical book (1942) about this Adventurer's Fen than he did in being a medic. Then in 1940 the War Agricultural Committee took over, drained it within an inch of its life and for the second time it became intensively cropped. Now the wheel has turned again, and once more it is becoming wilderness – this time by design. Some of the old folk in the village who had sweated to keep this land dry enough to farm were appalled when the National Trust revealed what it intended to do with the land it had bought. We all like our benchmarks to stay as we have known them, and as we think them permanent. But they are not, and don't.

Those old folk who shook their heads would not have appreciated the herd of little Konik ponies that now rove and roam on this soil. Hardy beasts that are used to wetland, they come from the farmland east of the River San in Poland, and descend from the tarpan, the prehistoric wild horse that roamed Britain and Europe since before the last Ice Age. The last pure tarpan died in Russia in 1879, but the Koniks share some of its genes and some of its features, like a dun coat and a black dorsal stripe. They are breeding well. Indeed, the stallions are competing as stallions should, and won the accolade of a excitable headline in the *Daily Mail* in 2016:

WILD HORSES COULDN'T DRAG THEM AWAY: BATTLE-SCARRED STALLIONS SNAPPED SPARRING IN THE CAMBRIDGESHIRE WETLANDS

Spring

The rare Konik ponies confronted each other on the wetlands of Wicken Fen Nature Reserve in Cambridgeshire. Stallions become frisky at this time as mares come into season and males bear the scratches from battling to breed. The fight lasted for several minutes as the stallions vied to show their dominance and were watched by three foals.

We watched a leggy foal watching impatiently while its dam had a nice satisfying roll on her back. Then, as she got up it demanded suck, but she walked on. Now clearly cross, the foal simply put his head under hers and its neck across her breast as she walked, and stopped her importunately in her tracks. Three times this happened, and then she gave in, with the foal flicking its tail in delight as he guzzled the rich milk, butting his muzzle against her belly.

Soon enough, we turned for home and duty. For an hour or so the world had been a long way away and something deep, atavistic perhaps, had been awake. But you can't live in dreams or memories. One by one the usual markers of routine were weakening, disappearing. All church services stopped, in the middle of Lent that we were seriously trying to keep properly; then all churches locked, including even the tiny church in the village where on most mornings at the end of my walk I used to go and say Mattins. Hector the black Labrador used to come with me: a pious dog, for whom I never bought a dog-collar. Thoughts of the other 'now' return. Perhaps this is a providential time to draw breath, to stop and think, and in this enforced staying at home, an unanticipated dose of what for a monk would be *stabilitas loci,* to read and meditate, to make electronic contact with friends whom we have not seen – and probably will not see – for some time. Change is in the air – literally, in the air. For a day or two I could not think what was, well, different, could not think of what I was being reminded. And then I realised. This extraordinary clarity of the light, which many people have independently noted, this silence – it is exactly what the world was like when I was young and first came here. And that the air is cleaner is true. Hardly any planes are scoring the sky with their contrails, and whether cheap air travel, environmentally prodigally costly, can (or should) ever return is a question not easy of confident answer. Air pollution worldwide is 50% less that it was this time last year. Today's news tells me India's electricity use has fallen to the lowest in 5 months 'due to lockdown.' The skies over China are clear for the first time in more than a generation. Anyone under 25 in China will see a sight they have never been before, a sky blue by day and full of stars at night. Even here: last night Venus dazzled as I have only ever seen her before in a desert sky in America, yet the moon was in its gibbous phase three days off the full. And other things: dolphins and fish return to the waters round Venice where they have not been seen for years. And there is a real spirit of cooperation and generosity about – at least in the necks of the woods I know.

I think we might be on the brink of a paradigm shift: certainly nothing will be the same again, and the fragile hollowness of the acquisitive and economic models that have ruled us for so long is clear as day to anybody who thinks at all. The quiet wisdom of Gaia may, just may, be listened to. The old tramlines are not there any more, though some will try to pretend they are, and they may be powerful enough, or their promises seductive enough, to get people to try to rebuild the old patterns. For the devil you know... There will be a cost.

⸺●⸺

Michael's son Will, who has pretty much taken over the farm now, is moving his sheep today from the field down the fen where they have been eating down what over the winter had grown on last year's stubbles. These sheep are so used to being moved around his scattered fields by trailer that they seem almost to be queuing up for the next bus when the first few are taken off to the new pasture. Heaven knows where he is going to put them, though, for there is hardly a bite of grass anywhere in this dry April: no rain for nearly four weeks and he is still having to give them hay. The sun is warm, the breeze gentle. The first shy flowers of the hawthorn – exceptionally early this year – are just opening, and a gentle green is breaking the buds on the willows. Field maple leaves are half out, with delicate pink scales shielding the lime green of the young leaves. A perfect day, they call it. Not when you are looking for a bite of spring grass and your stock of hay is running low. And where are the bees, who used to be so loud at this time of year in the first of the spring flowers? A solitary bumble is investigating the purple trumpets of the dead nettle.

Will's sheep – a bit of a mixture, some looking like pure Suffolks, a few showing the elaborate Southdown hairdo, and some simply dead common – are very lucky, for he looks after them with loving care, and when his rams' job is done – a week or so's orgy each year – those boys live on the fat of the land for the rest of the year. I suppose they enjoy their yearly indulgence: yet the pre-mounting panting does not seem to be accompanied by any passion, and I have seen ewes continuing to munch while it is going on. But ewes can get passionate about their lambs, and will stamp their feet and make for you menacingly, moving their lowered heads from side to side if you come too close. The nearest to passion I ever saw in rams was three Texel rams standing in a field doing nothing. Then two of them decided they did not like each other. And charged – if the lumbering gait can be so described – head to head. Their frontal bones met with – well, yes, a sickening thud. (There is quite some kinetic energy in 200 pounds of ram, even if its speed is modest.) They both looked dazed for a moment, and thought about it. Then they reversed, and did it again. And again. Slowly. By this time, clearly, nobody was winning, so they had a bite of grass, and then, by common consent joined forces and butted the non-combatant against the fence. For quite a time. Then they all got bored.

I am intrigued by the dynamics of flocks and herds. Though it is quite clear that the group can work together, and apparently arrive at a collective decision – it's time to move on, or let's all graze facing the same way – it is also quite clear that they have their likes and dislikes. Horse friendships are obvious: you'll see two friends standing motionless, nose to tail, on a summer dusk, occasionally flicking their tails to keep the flies moving. When he was turned out in the field with Albert's old cob, fat as butter with good feeding and no exercise (for Albert did not ride any more), the first horse we had struck up an immediate friendship with him and they whinnied with distress when separated and snickered with delight when they were reunited. But the next horse that Mariner was with – well, they just stood at opposite ends of the field ignoring each other. Dogs too have friends, doggy and otherwise, and, very obviously, dislikes. But transfer this to a herd, and it's something more hierarchical, like a pecking order among domestic hens. There is always one cow, or one bullock, away on its own. There is always one sheep that nobody seems to want to have in the flock. The outcast...

Once, in Iona one September, we were sitting on the first rise of the hill overlooking the machair. The sheep were quietly grazing that rich sward, all except one. She was down on the beach, grazing on the tidewrack, all alone. Suddenly, for no obvious reason, the flock by common consent decided they too would go to the beach – but not to the part where the solitary sheep was getting her dose of iodine. The leader – there is always a leader in any herd – set off, and the others all fell into line behind her, about 50 or 60 in all. She set off at a good trot, and when she came to the little sandy cliff where the tide and wind have eaten into the machair, some four or five feet, she took a graceful flying leap onto the beach.

The others followed with a regularity almost enough to put an observer to sleep. But they had to pass about 50 yards away from the solitary sheep on the beach. They ignored her, but not she them. She called to them, and they still ignored her. They speeded up, in a long line, galloping along the tidemark, making for the very furthest corner of the bay. Who knows why? What did they know was there? The lone sheep followed them, far, far behind, for it was clear she was lame, and moving was painful. As she drew near the flock, they began to move on again. 'We don't want anything to do with you...' Was it because she was lame, and somewhere deep in their instinct was the recognition that if the flock had to run from a predator, she would have been a liability? I don't know. But I do know she was 'unhappy'.

People in a crowd can be like that. We have herd instincts too, and some people make money and power from them.

I had noticed Will was moving his sheep when I was up early that morning. For I had work to do across the Fen, in Ely, and best to get there as soon as possible. (If you are going to have to be in a town, Ely is as good as they come.) The road across the Fen – well, some hate it, some love it. It started as a single-lane concrete road put in by the War Agricultural Committee in 1940. 'That's when we got the good roads, when the WarAg ran things', one old farmworker once said to me. For he had grown up when there were only unmetalled droves across the peat, and of course in winter they were impassable.

In a wet winter, farms in the Fen might be cut off for months. Sometimes the water was so high that in some cottages you had to make the kitchen fire on a bed of bricks to raise it above the inches of water on the floor. Good roads they were then, perhaps, but peat dries out, and not all at the same rate, and then gets wet again, and the concrete cracks, and so quite soon you have a road anything but level. Then try and put tarmac on it, and make it smoother, at least, with that. But the inexorable shrink/expand cycle goes on, and farm machinery and lorries get bigger and bigger and do more and more damage, and so you end up with a road that can, to oddballs like me, be exhilarating, and to others like my daughter-in-law who grew up in the flat silt country of Holland be sheer torture. In really wet weather, with great sheets of water coming up under the wheels from the deep puddles in the hollows, and with the motion of the car, it can be rather like being in a small boat in a choppy bit of sea.

Be all that as it may. The road runs first past the land the National Trust is rewilding, and then through some intensively farmed land, before it reaches the bank of the Cam and its wide washes, and climbs up to higher and solider ground. I know it very well. And I know those who live there almost with the familiarity of friends – though they are certainly oblivious of my kindly feelings. For the deer, whom I almost always see at about the same spot, only know me as a car whose lurching approach is to be avoided. The few hares sometimes test my brakes. At about the same spot I nearly always see a kestrel, often perched alert on the electricity wires. I regularly see a sparrowhawk – once I disturbed her and she took off with talons grasping a half eviscerated blackbird. (Yes, male and female sparrowhawks do look different: the musket has a blue-grey back, while Mrs is brown). There is a buzzard who has a favourite telegraph pole; once he killed almost in front of my wheels and I had to swerve. As I drive through the hamlet, I know that on the corner I shall have to watch out for duck. Once there was one fast asleep, head under wing, in the middle of the road, and when I stopped and honked at her she woke up with a very bad grace. And then, by the tumbledown old chapel so enveloped in ivy that most people now do not even know it was ever there, and that once it had a congregation in its corrugated iron, Gothic-windowed erstwhile glory, there is the cock pheasant.

I think he is an old bird, for I have seen one there with identical markings and habits for at least three years. But how he has lived so long is a mystery. For, especially in spring, when a young (or old) bird's fancy lightly turns, etc., he will sit in the shorter grass at road's verge, and as the car comes round the bend – I drive quite slowly – he will get up, and start to run along the road in the same direction as the car. Now, to his left he has a wide open field, surely inviting to a pheasant as a means of escape. But no: every time, as soon as I draw level and am about to overtake, he flies in front of the car. Nor does he just cross to the other side, or rocket up as pheasants do. He flies along the road, at the same height as the windscreen, straining every muscle, until he will suddenly tire and collapse into the verge on the same side he just left. Not quite a suicide wish, perhaps, but certainly a bird-brained version of playing 'chicken'.

———————•———————

L ate March: Good Friday is early this year, for Easter falls on the first full moon after the spring equinox, and there are two full moons in this month. (Once in a blue moon… what happens if you put a comma after 'Once'?) The sickle of the new moon cut the sky on March 17. We are only 4 days after Lady Day, properly the Feast of the Annunciation to the Blessed Virgin Mary, another of the Quarter Days. The Fen is sodden with all the rain that keeps sweeping in from the North Sea. When wind sets in the north-east with rain, we know, here, we are in for a soak. Neither ash not oak is yet moving, though, so I can't use the old country prognostication for the summer:

'Oak before ash, only a splash.
Ash before oak, wait for a soak.'

Last night it did clear up, and when I took Hector out for his last sniff, widdle and squat before bed the moon was out, gibbous, with a halo of ice crystals round it: sure sign of more rain on its way. (The circle is 15 degrees of arc from the moon: roughly a handspan as you look at it.) The night was quite still: the day's mean wind had dropped. A month ago and the wild geese would have been noisy: now many of them – but by no means all – have begun their flight north and the sky is quiet of the beat of their wings and their calling to keep in formation. The silence was momentarily broken by the muntjac barking about half a mile away and the call of a barn owl hunting along the river. (Their call makes small animals freeze.) He (she?) would have been kept in by all this wet, for their flight feathers have soft, fimbriate – comb-like, fringed – edges, which allows them to move in ghostly silence on the wing. But such feathers do not repel rain and a long wet spell when they have not had good hunting can be a disaster.

Today dawned bright, a sky pale blue, and the sun rose into a day too bright to last: the sort of brightness that tells you that you will have thickening cloud in an hour and rain in three. And we have, in buckets – and from time to time *comme une vache qui pisse* – I love that expression, for it is exact in its onomatopoeic splashiness.

But while it was bright in the sky, and dry above, even if sodden underfoot, I was out with Hector well before most people were stirring. A day like this is for the wide skies of the Fen, so although we come out of the gate and he turns left to go up to the hill, which is his favourite walk, I turn right down the lane. After a wistful pause, head on one side, ears cocked, he shrugs, 'All right, then,' and sets off at a slow trot. He is an agreeable fellow who usually sees my point of view. He reads his newspaper, checks who has been and peed on this bit of grass, whose scent is here, what was the track of this muntjac: he sniffs at the tufts of grass which look much one like another to humans, but which clearly are not, he ignores the neighbour's cat which curses him from a silent, tense and baleful crouch, and after much fastidious choosing of a spot stuffs his head into the hedge so he cannot be recognised, sticks his bottom out and squats. I have never persuaded him to do it the other way round, which would be more convenient for everyone.

Good Friday was for countryfolk round here the day you planted your spuds. It's a big job, and when you had a large family to feed you needed to plant a lot. Some say that the tradition started because cottagers were working so hard that Good Friday was the only day between New Year and Easter that they had free to get into their garden to start planting.

For a variety of reasons, we have just got a new allotment. It needs breaking in, and spuds are a good cleaning and breaking in crop. The land has been neglected for years. The previous people covered it in sheeting to stop weeds, which has worked... except that the thick white roots of convolvulus, a most pernicious and hungry weed, everywhere vein the heavy clay beneath the sheeting. Every time you touch them they break, and any tiny bit you leave can be a huge plant in merely weeks. There are very few worms – not a good sign. For the plot is on that hummock of Kimmeridge clay that forms the Isle of Ely, a clay that runs from the crumbling cliffs of Dorset to the Wash and out into the North Sea. In some places it is full of fossils – Jurassic – and there are ammonites and cycads and lots of the extinct oyster *gryphaea,* commonly known about here as Devil's toenails. I have found them sometimes in large numbers, concreted together – very much as you find slipper limpets now. Though in the US *Crepidula fornicata* is known as the 'fornicating slipper snail', its morals are actually impeccable: when groups of individuals are often found heaped up and fastened together, the larger, older females are below and the smaller, younger males on top. But as a heap grows, the males turn into females (making them sequential hermaphrodites.) I think the adjective *fornicata* has more to do with the arched back of the snail than with sexual abandon. For it was under the arches, *fornices,* of the aqueducts that Roman ladies of the night plied their trade.

This is cruel, hard land to dig, and you need something to muse on, however irrelevant, when you are doing that repetitive thrust with the right foot, levering out of the spit, and casting it so it falls upside down on the turned earth in front of you. My back is complaining at the unaccustomed strain, for by contrast the land at the house is rich, deep, well worked. I am beginning to wonder if it was wise to take this patch on. The land is wet, wet, wet, and drains very badly. Idly, I wonder if the climate has yet warmed enough to grow rice. As I dig, I try to turn each heavy spit so that it falls cleanly off the spade – but it doesn't, it sticks like glue, and the spade has to be scraped.

Water: it made and still dominates this landscape I know so well. I am not just talking about this grey clay, laid down over millennia in a tropical sea, but about the Fens that surround the Isle and stretch far to the north. Once, when Doggerland joined this land to the continent and the North Sea's grey waves were still far off to the north, where now is Fen was forest, forest of oak and beech and pine and yew. Red deer roamed widely – big animals, and if the 5000-year-old antler hanging on my wall, which was cast by one that roamed that forest is anything to go by, bigger than is now usual. But as the warming earth melted the ice, the sea began to claim the land. 65 feet below Ordnance Datum, all round the coast and out into the North Sea, you can find traces of the Old Forest, and fishermen's nets bring up the bones of aurochsen and antlers of deer and the tools of the men who hunted them. The rising water table in the flattish basin where many of the larger rivers of England converge before discharging their water into the sea gradually made what is now the Fens more and more waterlogged, and few trees can stand having their feet always paddling in water. Water killed the old forest well before Roman times. It is hard to imagine the leafless, lifeless forest, with gaunt skeleton trees against the sky. Some say they were all blown down in a chaos of tangled, snapped branches, by a single great storm some 5000 years ago, for many of them lie in the same direction, as if the wind came from the north-west. (In the mornings after the Great Storm of 1987 I saw something similar in the woods in Norfolk, the shallow roots of beech and oak not able to hold onto the light soil as the wind pummelled them. At Wandlebury Ring, a hill fort on that is the nearest thing to a hill within cycling distance of Cambridge, the much-loved beeches, planted as saplings when America was still a colony, went down like skittles.)

Where the dead trees lay on the waterlogged earth, over centuries a bed of peat many feet thick grew to cover them in their sleep. It covered too the bones of animals and the habitations of men, like Must Farm; it covered the antlers the red deer cast each spring – like the one I call mine, on the wall by the stairs. The rivers, Ouse and Nene, Cam, and Welland, already slow, became sluggish, meandered, spread, and flooded as they could not get rid of their water into the rising sea. Water plants, sedges, mosses, reeds, little water-loving trees like alder and osier, grew and died and rotted into rich dark mould. Century after century the peat thickened, and the big trees slept in their anaerobic blanket, gradually turning into 'bog oaks', best firing of all, and heavy and hard as iron to a man's saw when they dry out. Many is the time in the first years we were in this house when we sweated sawing up oak for the fire, and I kicked myself for letting it get too dry before we did so. For sharpening and setting a saw is tedious work, and a long two-handed saw takes time.

The wetland became the haunt of innumerable birds and fish, and men made a good living. Not only did the fen provide fuel – and I knew older people who still could handle a turf becket and cut their winter peat – but also summer grazing for sheep, and very valuable fisheries, and in winter seemingly limitless supplies of waterfowl. Every bit of the fen was used, and parishes jealously guarded their rights of grazing and fowling and turbary in their patch – sometime separated by quite a few miles from the actual parish. The birds were trapped, either by baiting hooks – again, done within living memory, just – or by decoys; later, they were gunned down in hundreds at a shot with punt guns. Here there was a substantial trade in waterfowl with Cambridge and, from the fens generally, with London itself. Species we would now go miles to see through expensive binoculars graced many a table: ruffs and reeves, godwits, larks, swans, snipe, and all the tribes of ducks and geese. One of the reasons why there was so much local opposition to the draining of the fens from the XVIIth century onwards was precisely because these resources, and the common rights, enabled the poor to live, if not in comfort, with at least a fire and a fowl to cook on it. Enclosure, and Parliament's insistence (to its credit) on some land being set aside as allotments – my own was on just such a patch, and still administered by the body set up by the Enclosure Commissioners – was no compensation. Enclosure, as John Clare, who was one of its victims, witnesses in his poems, was a disaster for the poor, hastening their slide into being simply paupers. But without it, and the agricultural and economic forward planning it allowed, the new industrial towns could not have been fed.

Things are never simple. I thought they were, once upon a time.

———————— • ————————

So much has been written about the draining the Fens, and the constant battle with water when they had been drained. Most of the people I knew who remembered those real hard times have now gone. Farms in the Fen were often set on the patches of higher ground, or, as the peat dried out and shrank, on the roddons, or former river channels, slightly firmer, slightly higher, where there was some gravel or chalk brought down by a sometime stream. Even so, a normal winter could mean you did not get out of the Fen for several weeks except by punt, and my neighbour Ray remembered a year in his childhood – his family lived down in the deepest Fen, where the land has shrunk to below sea level – when the punt cleared the barbed wire of the fences as they ferried the hay (pray God it lasts out!) to the cattle enisled on a patch of higher ground.

Spring 1947, and a rapid thaw after one of the coldest and snowiest winters of the century brought the accumulated wet of months pouring out of the counties of central England into the Fen basin. The vast area of washes between the Old and New Bedford Rivers held it, just, but it ponded back up the tributary drains and rivers, until came the night in March when, swollen by torrential rain, and held back by the equinoctial spring tides, the highest of the year, all the major rivers burst their banks. Many of the embankments had been built way back in the 17th century by Cornelius Vermuyden, as part of the huge Fenland drainage led by the Duke of Bedford: they had stood much, but this they could not. Thousands of acres were swamped, half of it prime arable land desperately needed to supply a population only just getting over the War. Winter wheat and huge quantities of planted potatoes were submerged. The force of the water pouring through a weak place made even a small breach a big one in no time. It washed away fences, knocked down doors, destroyed walls, even those of brick. People in the deep Fen saw their homes flooded to first floor level, or bungalows submerged; hundreds were homeless. Pigs, cattle, sheep and poultry drowned in their thousands.

One of the worst breaks was just across the Fen from this house, fifteen minutes easy drive now on a road whose bumpiness never lets you forget the unreliability of peat and whose horizon is bounded by the banks of the straightened rivers. Young Albert, whose parents Kate and Albert had half of this house, remembered his father calling him from his bed that night – he would have been about 20 – to get his clothes on quick: the two of them cycled in the heavy rain, their clothes getting heavier and heavier with the water, across this Fen, praying that they would get to the higher land before the banks holding this little river burst – for even in this fen the river runs high above the fields. When they got to the big breach they joined the hundreds of men and boys trying desperately to stem the water, while a lighter full of gault clay dug from Roswell Pits at Ely was held against the bank to lessen the force of the great cascade. When the tide went down thirty miles to the north and the overcharged rivers could vent themselves, the pressure eased, but another twelve hours would bring another high tide. Albert filled bag after bag, day after day, dog-tired, with the sticky gault clay. The clear-up took years.

Francis Grose's *Provincial Glossary* (1787), records the local saying,
'The bailiff of Bedford is coming'. The Ouse, or Bedford river, is in Cambridgeshire called the bailiff of Bedford; because, when swoln with rain in the winter-time, by overflowing, it carries off the cattle, &c. on the Isle of Ely and adjacent low grounds; so that this saying was a warning to drive off the cattle, &c. lest they should be distrained by the bailiff of Bedford; i.e. the river Ouse. By draining the fens, this bailiff's power has been superseded

Or so they had thought. Yet wise Vermuyden had suggested in 1639 that a Cut Off Channel, to run through Norfolk and Suffolk to catch the headwaters of the Wissey, Lark and Little Ouse and take them to Denver was necessary to the strategy of his overall plan. Nothing was done. John Rennie dusted the idea off again in 1810, but the cost was prohibitive. Finally, floods in 1937 and 1939, and the disaster of 1947, made it happen. In summer the Channel is a quiet place, between deep banks, its still waters mirroring the dragonflies and damsel flies, and its deeps the haunt of deep-keeled bream and cogitating, slow carp. 'They' forbid bathing, but people do. And ingeniously, its water is part of the drinking water supply water for Essex.

It is hard not to think of those floods, and the constant struggle to keep the land dry, when I see, as I did on my walk this morning, the water lying in broad shallow patches where the National Trust are re-wilding the land the turf farmer almost stripped of its ancient, mushroom-opulent soil. I can understand why the older generation of people who had grown up in this part hated all the Trust was doing: it was, in a way, breaking faith with their people. Yet it is ironic that only a half dozen or so generations back, those ancestors were fighting hard, even using physical violence, to *stop* the drying of the Fens. But nothing is for ever. One day the Fen will be water from horizon to horizon.

True, on the whole the Cam, and the Ouse, and the Welland, and the Nene, have been taught to behave themselves. But I once knew a man who as a small child in 1920 had been taken from Cambridge in a horse-drawn chaise by his parents to see an exceptionally high tide on the Cam at Waterbeach. (This was of course long before the present Denver Sluice was built.) He saw a tiny tidal bore – he told me it was about two inches high – sweep past. For the Cam is naturally tidal that far upstream. So far, only that far. But with rising sea levels the future is certain. You can glimpse that future in a wet winter when the tide holds back the water and the Washes are full:

water as far as the eye can see, the willows on the banks seeming to enjoy paddling in it, and the hosts of migrant duck and geese from the Northlands, and swans from far Russia, for whom this is heaven-sent, a holiday.

———●———

On the Trust land, round the edge of the flashes, driven by the wind, is a miniature tidemark, full of rich pickings – small creatures drowned, invertebrates, small mammals – for hungry scavengers, even for foxes. A couple of furlongs away, a few greylags are feeding, one goose, as always, alert, on guard. Near me an uncertain skylark went up and came down again pretty quickly: 'Is this the time to look for a mate? Or to warn people off? No: too cold.' Not a bad song to come out of eating worms, insects, spiders and slugs.

A coot chacks as it comes out of the reeds on the little mere the National Trust has made to attract waterfowl and dragonflies. As I come round the side of the stand of young wood – it is really not much more than a scrubby thicket yet – there are three roe deer grazing, a hundred yards away. Sudden, their heads are up, and they look at me with that surprised, slightly offended, pose deer manage so easily, ears cocked. A buck in velvet and two does. Not frightened, they just walk along as I do, and even when they see the dog, they take only a bound or two before they stop, look back again. They are curious, and circle round ahead of me – they know that now they have me and the dog between them and the village, rather than the potential danger of the other way about.

Jackdaws have taken over the owl box on the Hythe by the river. I like jackdaws, cheerful fellows with a sense of humour. Or so it seems. Two egrets are gravely hunting, pacing along the river bank. They have only been seen here in the last few years. Are they a pair? I keep seeing them together. Perhaps they are just good friends. There is the usual morning heron in the field. The other morning as the kissing gate clanked closed behind me three got up with that slow beat of their great wings – which carries them surprisingly fast – and call out 'Frank!' to me. Which is not my name, but what can you expect?

———◆———

Two formally clipped yews flank the entrance to the study. I planted them when we first came here, and they must be about ten or fifteen years younger than I am. Mere infants, as yews go, who will I hope see many springs. For me too, this is another spring: and this one has a Significant Birthday in it – though if you comfortingly put my age in Celsius I could claim I am only in my 20s. As a very old lady, well into her 80s, said to me, when I really was in my 20s, 'Dear boy, I am still young and beautiful inside, you know.' True enough, and life does not get less interesting as knees get stiffer. But each spring has something more of the whisper of autumn in it as you get older, and the sense of urgency, if anything, increases. Perhaps it should: for by now not everything matters, but some things do, terribly.

This spring, though, the season has seemed to feel no urgency. April: weeks of dry weather, bright sun, with an unrelenting stiff north wind, dropping to give often hard frosts each night. The coldest for 60 years, they say. (What was I doing, that cold spring 60 years ago?) Ground dried as hard as concrete – the clods of soil on our clay allotment are painful to walk on. Plants struggling to get going. Drapes of fleece each night on the vulnerable tips of the new spuds, seedling tomatoes brought into the relative warmth of the living room (as our friends know, this is not exactly a hot house), where they strain leggily towards the window. Buds on the trees stalled, half out, even at the end of the month. No new growth on the yews, which usually by this time I am getting ready to clip. Insect life sparse, migrant birds late arriving – perhaps the north wind held them back. It's been such a contrast with the warm mellowness of the Coronavirus spring last year. And now suddenly we are in a May that has brought the wet, to be sure, but in deluges, with rioting westerly winds which would do March proud. In a few days most of the trees have shot out their leaves to try to catch up with all the photosynthesising they have missed (there will be narrow rings this year), yet here we are, still waiting for the ash leaves finally, from their black shields, to catch up with the purple flowers which come first. The oaks are only just shyly putting on their mantle of bright green, and we are only five weeks from the solstice. A fortnight late, today we saw that my beloved swifts, whom I look for each May 6, had at last returned to the village. I had a sudden happy lift to the heart as they wheeled high above the garden. But strange weather, and stranger each year.

It so chanced that in that first week of sun and storm business – in fact, it was about this book – took me over to the Marches. We found a lodge to stay in, greenly hidden in the heart of a big wood of oak and beech and hazel, ash and yew and sycamore. The wood had once been clear felled, in 1914 or so, to make pit props and revetments and the other wooden things the maw of war demands. The trees, waiting their time as stool and seed and nut and acorn, have come back, straight and tall. They have grown close together as they would in a young wildwood, so the trunks are long and straight with few low branches, and the ground beneath is deep in tree litter. Someone has recently very neatly cropped a couple of oaks, which were lying stretched out by their neatly trimmed stools. They look like mere youths in their slimness, but I counted the rings of one and made it well over 80. And their succeeding springs are measured in the width of the rings, and I thought I could see the traumatic harshness of 1940-41, 46-47, 62-3, and the Great Drought of 1976 when I was far away in a land where the sun never sets in summer and the only trees are fossils in the coal.

But the living trees in the wood sang in the wind, they sang us to sleep, sang us awake, their low *cantus firmus* punctuated by the melismata of the birds' spring songs. The shelter the wood gave allowed the luxuriance of fern, the uncurling of the elaborate croziers of bracken, the sudden delight of low growing herb Robert or campion or bluebell. This large wood reminds of the woods our distant ancestors knew, before the land was plotted and pieced into field and furrow, and tamed by hedges.

Time in hand… or rather, 'let's play hookey for a couple of days before back to work and teaching.' Playing hookey always adds a stolen spice to pleasure… So we church-crawled, wandering from Norman to Saxon, with an occasional foray into the high Middle Ages, and thus made, or in some cases remade, our acquaintance with some notable yews who could remember the ancient woods the Saxons knew.

They used to tell me that yews were planted in churchyards because of the need for longbows. But longbows were often made of ash. Then they told me that it was so that the stock did not eat their poison, and you kept stock out of the churchyard. But before lawnmowers, geese and sheep were often grazed in the churchyard. And yews grow in hedgerows which fringe where stock graze, and you don't see cattle or sheep making beelines for them. Whatever… the fact is that some churchyards do hold some venerable old trees, some few so old that they go back before there were churches in this land. The Fortingall yew in Glen Lyon in Scotland could be anything from over two thousand to nine thousand years old. One legend says Pontius Pilate was born under this tree and played as a child in its branches. (If true, one wonders what his high born mother thought she was doing…) But when the Faith came, often the churches were planted where the land was already sacred, a precinct of the gods, and some yews may have been there already. For in folklore they are connected with death and resurrection, the unending cycle.

I have planted yews in my time, as I said, and these decades-old youngsters in the garden in the village have pupped, and their children have grown from the scarlet berries, as red as the lips of La Belle Dame Sans Merci, to sturdy striplings themselves. The thick, dark, windproof shade of the space inside a yew tree is home to many insects, and outside the study door one of that pair I first planted holds a blackbird's nest each year and the other offers a residence to a wren. But these are nothing compared to the massive corpulence of the yews of Dymock, which Robert Frost and Edward Thomas knew, or the great yew at Kempley which may have seen the plaster being mixed for the base of the paintings with which a forgotten twelfth century artist brought the church to colourful life. Old friends for me, not for my Lady, to whom I introduced them, and it was a joy to run a hand over their bark. We sat on the bench inside the yew at Much Marcle. The hard, grained wood showed the smoothing of centuries of hands, the cut marks of knife and chisel point, and a tiny flourish of green leaves grew inside at the edge of a little hole that pierced the outer shell and let in the light. He (I think of yews as 'he') seemed to like us sitting there, while he sighed at the wind in his branches and the rain bounced on the path outside. So too I have sheltered inside the great yew at Martindale church near Ullswater, also a place of comfort. It is estimated to have been a sapling when Martindale knew no Norse name but was in Welsh speaking Rheged. The men of Martindale, famous archers, are documented as having cut their bow staves from this tree.

My honorary uncle's vicarage was in the clayey drumlin country just south of Kendal. I loved going there as a child, and remember with utter clarity the room I had, its chintz curtains, the smell of breakfast cooking as I woke up, and the big yew just outside the window which broke the stiff winds of the west off the Irish Sea into sough and sigh. It sang me to sleep more than once, and I loved it, I loved climbing up into its welcome, I loved the soft, yielding carpet of old needles underneath it, that rarely got wet. (A tramp I once knew told me that yews were the most comfortable trees to sleep under. I have never had to, but I am sure he was right.) Years upon years later, when my beard was beginning to be flecked with grey, I went back to that house on the hill, and someone had cut down My Tree to build a prefabricated concrete garage. Felled, all felled… as if a friend who could have lived for many more lives of men had been murdered. The only recognition of the rural setting these new owners had managed was a full size fibreglass cow, black and white like a Holstein, save where green lichen was growing on its back.

Back to work. I shall plant a few more trees next autumn, and, indeed, I know where two nice little yew seedlings are hiding.

———— • ————

Saturday: my usual day for the bigger outside jobs. But not this time, for this is another day of cold driving rain, and with the wind setting where it is and the look in the sky, we have another six or seven hours of this. So I stay in, and write these sentences… A wet dog fox crosses the garden, purposeful. Ten minute later a vixen looks in at the French window of the study where I am writing what I always hope might be deathless prose, sees Hector lying there, and backs away: 'So sorry: I am intruding.' Hector was fast asleep. Now a cock blackbird beaded with wet is foraging for whatever is eatable – they are pretty catholic in taste – below the yew outside the door. At least he gets a bit of shelter there. Years ago I had Fred, my tame one, who used to follow me round the garden and on occasion would perch on my hand to take a titbit, his head cocked so that one of his orange-rimmed eyes could look straight into mine. But only when he had young to feed. After that – after what was sometimes the third brood of the year – he would startle away with his loud descending cry of alarm.

The dog still needs to go out, whatever the weather. Rain does not bother him, though it ruins the ground scent, and he rubs his wet fur against my legs to dry off when we get home (and to thank me for his walk, I think). Walking makes you think, reflect, remember, project. With a companion you can't resist the temptation to talk, and then if you notice things you have to interrupt yourself, or indeed them. (Neither is comfortable.) You think, with all this rain, what will it be like come harvest? and then, what it *was* like come harvest. My mind flicks back to an August day in a quieter world, soon after we came here. For I must be one of the last men alive to have seen a field with stooked sheaves reaching up the hill to the horizon, and to have seen old Ambrose's Suffolk Punches pulling the plough in the fen between Ely and Stuntney, turning the stubbles of the year before, bleached by the winter, into the richness of the black fen for the next crop.

———•———

For the first time for weeks, the wind has gone westerly: SSW, warm, a bit boisterous. A bright day. The sort of day one expects of April. There is more rain on the way, but after weeks of it, at last, today, the birds can get on with things, and this morning when I took the dog out, there was activity all round, and after the almost silent weeks a riot of song. A starling, (cheerful fellows: no wonder Mozart loved his pet starling and gave it an elaborate funeral) keeps flying onto the telephone wire from the corner of the roof, inside which I think he and Mrs must be building a nest. I feel I want to call him Papageno. But that would be the wrong way round.

The ash buds are suddenly not dour black, tightly closed, but are lightening, beginning to burst. And first to appear are tight bunches of purplish florets: male and female flowers typically grow on different trees, though a tree can bear male and female flowers on different branches. The sticky horse chestnut buds have already flaunted the startling bright green of their new leaves to the sun, and the hedgerow blackthorns, white over like new snow, promise a bounty of bitter sloes come September. Bird song at dawn is insistent, urgent: 'Get *up*! Get *up*!' says the blackbird, and woodpigeon tells Susie off again, while greenfinch creaks out his *glissando*, like a rusty hinge. Speedwell's blue outstares the sky from the sward at my feet. In the vegetable garden the seeds are sending up tentative green shoots to test the air. The wind is combing the river into a wrinkle of smiles.

Christina Rossetti is one of the poets who knew perfectly the heart-breaking beauty of spring that I see:

There is no time like Spring,
Like Spring that passes by;
There is no life like Spring-life born to die, –
Piercing the sod,
Clothing the uncouth clod,
Hatched in the nest,
Fledged on the windy bough,
Strong on the wing:
There is no time like Spring that passes by,
Now newly born, and now
Hastening to die.

My friend Ron has an acre or two in the old quarry. He is the chap who has the sheep I sometimes lean over the gate and try to talk to. Those sheep live in the lap of luxury, but sheep never look as if they are enjoying it much. Except for the lambs, who are always fun. (But grow up to be sheep.) I met two very young ones on my walk early this morning. They stared at me, and the bright low sun shone through their pricked ears, making them pink. For what must have been over a minute we stood, motionless, silent. The little ram lamb decided this was all too boring, did a little jump, and butted his companion. I was clearly dismissed.

Today, before breakfast: the first brood of moorhen chicks, little balls of black fluff almost running along the surface of the stream to catch up with anxious tail-flicking Mummy. A couple of buzzards mewing to each other as they ride the easy wind in huge circles, a stately dance. (Later, I see one perched on a fence post.) In the garden, a furious blackbird cock sees off a jay. Not a bad start to the day. But now it gets serious, for I have essays to read and students to teach. Not that I mind, really. As it happens, some of them have been writing on Chaucer's *Parliament of Fowls*.

Of the joyful sights of spring, and there are many, this one always lifts my heart. I know a farm where the owner loves his cattle as if he were their father. (I think that was said of William the Conqueror and his deer, but my friend is more pacific.) They are inside in the winter months, partly for their comfort and wellbeing and partly to rest the land, when it is at its wettest and softest, from the poaching of their feet, which can turn it in no time at all into a quagmire on which not a blade of grass will grow for months. He feeds them well: well made sweet-smelling hay, and something they really love, the silage he cuts out of the big cake of it covered in tarpaulins held down with old tyres to stop the covers blowing away in the winter gales. I love the smell of silage, its richness, its hint of molasses. And of course, as half-fermented grass, it's got a certain whiff of alcohol. That might be why the animals like it.

But there comes a day in spring, usually a dry and sunny one, when the new grass is showing its brighter green. Then the gate is opened and the animals are let out of the shelter. They stand cautiously at first by the way into the field, as if looking in disbelief at what is before them: space, and sky, and wind, and green. And then there is a rush, and they charge into the new grass, and low, and – a joyful sight if ever there was one – kick up their heels in delight. And do it again. And run, enjoying the space. And then, head down, and guzzle on the rich sweetness. (Oh yes, new grass is sweet. Try it. We can't digest the cellulose, but the sugars you can chew out if it are subtly flavoured, different for each variety.) And happiness abounds.

No rest for the farmer, though. If he no longer has to feed, he has the huge job of clearing out the yard's trodden and urine-soaked straw, of spreading the rotted manure on his land, where its richness – another grand country smell! – will make the ears fat on the wheat and barley, and the grass in its quiet alchemy will transmute its goodness into next year's hay.

———————◆◆———————

I am later than usual in the walk this morning, and don't really care, for I have got to that stage of University Term when things can just wait as everyone else will be behindhand too. I took in the river, for I was delighted to hear from Pam, who is Jess the melancholy deaf mongrel's owner, that our resident pair of swans have hatched their brood. But I don't see them. So up to the wood, at the edge of which I suddenly hear very cross jackdaws making a right fuss over a cruising buzzard. They see her off, though, with a spectacular display of combat flying. The bright day is warming up now, and in the shafts of sunlight coming through the canopy of the young wood, hosts of tiny insects scintillate. A spot of scarlet catches my eye: an early ladybird bright against the lichen on the bark of the maple.

'Seen a swallow yet?' says a cheerful Ron to me as I come up to the gate into his field. ('Ron's Meadow', a painted sign says proudly.) I know that tone means that he has, is delighted they are back, and even more delighted that he has beaten me to it. I acknowledge defeat. 'Just behind my house, two of them, this morning just after dawn.' We chat a bit, about this and that, about how the swallows are a bit earlier than usual this year, and about the frogspawn in the little pond he has made and into which the roof of his miniature shippon drains. His fat little Jack Russell gazes adoringly up at me. We have always got on well in all his fourteen years, and I am not in a hurry, not just at the moment.

The daffodils we planted are just about over – they come before the swallow dares and take the winds of March with beauty: a line of Shakespeare's that stuck in my mind for ever when I first heard it. The swallows used to arrive about April 21 – that was when I'd expect to see the first brave ones hawking after insects along the Cam, flickering over the pool by the Granta Inn or under the bridge at Queens' College, as I cycled to the Library, often muffled up against the east wind. They seem to get earlier each year as the world warms. My neighbour tells me she saw three exhausted ones, just arrived, at dawn the day before yesterday – actually before Ron did – on the wire of the fence round the field where she keeps her donkeys.

Every year there is a nest on a beam in the stable my son and I built, and we have to remember not to shut the top half of the door quite to, until all the young are fledged. (They can eat their own bodyweight of insects – 20gms – each day. Well done, swallows. Keep at it.) One of their favourite places in the village is in the lee of a stand of talkative tall poplars on the edge of the village, but where I love to watch them best is as they fly along just skimming, occasionally even touching, the water of the river. Insects collect there, in the lee of the banks, and later the bats will hawk along there as well. In fact, there comes a moment on a still summer evening, about 20 minutes after sunset as the light fades, when you are not quite sure whether it is swallows or bats you are seeing, and then, suddenly, you know they are bats. Once, decades ago, I could hear their shrill radar. Not now. The poor insects don't stand a chance, for a pipistrelle, our commonest kind, weighing in at up to 8 gms, can eat 3,000 bugs a night, about a third of their bodyweight. Almost as good as a swallow, and summer nights are short.

Under the roof of this old house there is that void, and all of ours that is up there are the header tanks for the water, some old carpets, a few old cases and a trunk that belong to my Great Aunt Florence. (My great aunts deserved capital letters.) Once it was suggested that we ought to clear it all out, but, well, we thought better of it, and decided that if the children were going to inherit… they could do it. In time. But lots of other creatures use it. Flies of various and regrettable sorts hibernate; once swifts used to nest there; and the sparrows over the years have made veritable haystacks in the corners by the eaves.

There was one year a spectacular wasp nest – they did not bother us, so we let them be. But the best of all was that for many springs, from about April, we had a pipistrelle maternity ward. For while a male bat will defend his special territory in the breeding season, the ladies get into a huddle together for the messy business of birth and rearing – and, one assumes, gossip as bats understand it. 'There he is, showing off that new territory, and thinks he's God's gift to all females. I knew him when he was little whippersnapper… Personally, dear, I never touch midges…' A researcher from the University Zoology Department – she said, ingenuously, when I had got her unusual name wrong for the third time, 'Just call me the batty lady' – used to come and sit on the lawn night after night at dusk counting the females as they came out from the gap between the soffit and the wall just like parachutists leaving a wartime glider. When the exodus started they were baling out at about four every minute, launching themselves into the buoyancy of air. One evening we counted 68 baling out, and then got tired. We felt honoured, for it was an exceptionally big roost. By late June or July the young are born, and the roost begins to disperse. But I liked to think that we had many of the same ladies back year after year – for pipistrelles do live a number of years, exceptionally as many as 12. Perhaps they had roosted there each early summer since the house was built.

I have never repaired that gap between the wall and the soffit.

———— • ————

An open space in the wood, where the ash dieback has let the light in, is this year spectacularly full of daisies: one of those unexpected things, and it won't be the same next year.

Chaucer has a poem where he casts himself as a contemplative figure gazing at the beauty of a daisy – it's one of those conventions which carried a lot of force then, which lots of writers and painters used, but which leaves most of us now cold. The daisy symbolised innocence, loyal love, beauty, patience and simplicity, it was one of Blessed Mary's flowers. But daisies, the humble nuisance on the lawns of some gardeners, are indeed worth a second, careful look. Their many florets surround the central disk, each a separate flower, not a petal, and the disk is itself made up of many more separate flowers. Look carefully, and you see their rich gold is laid out in two

Fibonacci spirals, one clockwise, and counterpointing anticlockwise. Magical. Modestly they close their eyes as night falls, true to their name in Old English, *daes eage*, 'day's eye.' They can, the old books say, slow bleeding, relieve indigestion, ease coughs, and supposedly ease an aching back, as 'the gardener's friend.' (Why am I so mean as to mow them on the lawn if they could be so good to me?) The leaves, they say, can make a tasty addition to salads, for they are closely related to artichokes. But it would take a long time to gather enough of their fleshy little leaves to get a decent mouthful.

Queen Anne's lace. I used to curse it, but now I love its delicate tracery of leaves and tall hollow stalk, and the froth of its umbels from early May to late June. Look at the flower heads carefully, and you see all the fractal patterns, the tiny insects feeding on the rich nectar, and you get the slightly aniseedy scent. You can even eat it. In some parts it used to be called 'mother die': the superstition was that if you brought it into the house your mother would die. Perhaps everyone in the village cursed it as a damn nuisance because there was some relic of that superstition behind their dislike. I did not know the plant before coming to this limy country, and saw it as they did, a pest to be got rid of. Which Queen Anne? Possibly Richard II's good queen, Anne of Bohemia, but it was a favourite flower of James I's Anne of Denmark, who challenged the ladies of her court to make a lace pattern based on it.

Others love it too: this afternoon we saw a female Orange Tip butterfly perched on an umbel to feed on its nectar. Her markings made her almost invisible.

The year 2020 was unseasonably warm: the first swallows arrived well before they usually come. Many things are waking up in this strange warmth. Hodge the cat brought in a grass snake. It was shamming dead, as they do. I suddenly noticed – why had this wonderful detail escaped me before? – the beautiful dark lilac colour of its open jaws as the sun caught them, its black forked tongue lolling out of its mouth like an undone bootlace. Its muscular body felt cool and supple as I picked it up and put it below a hedge where it could recover from the trauma of being thrown up into the air and caught. A quarter of an hour later it was gone. Later, I saw another, swimming across Reach Lode.

Rev. Leonard Jenyns, vicar of the next village but one in the 1840s, and the man who would have gone instead of his friend Darwin on HMS *Beagle* had the family living suddenly not fallen vacant, records,

'Snakes abound in our fens, where they sometimes attain a large size, occasionally measuring more than four feet in length. When surprised in such situations, they generally betake themselves to the water, in which element they not only swim freely, but have the power of remaining at the bottom for a long time without inconvenience…The snake is first generally seen abroad about the beginning of April; and on the 22nd of that month, I have found the sexes in copulation: during this act they are extended side by side in a straight line.'

He did not strike them with his stick, like Teiresias.

This morning, not for the first or last time, we had to get up and shut the bedroom window well before dawn. For the dawn chorus is at this time of year, and with the number of trees and shrubs round us, almost at the level of massed choirs. First a blackbird starts, while there is only a smudge of grey in the eastern sky. Then another, and another, all telling each other to keep away. On the topmost branch of the sycamore I planted on our boundary twenty years ago (and forgot about until suddenly I saw it was a big tree), a thrush pipes up, and by golly, he is a Pavarotti among thrushes. That sound fifteen yards from the window would wake the dead. Two cocks – I know both quite well – start up, one from the farmyard over the river, the other from just along the lane. Each is telling the other, needlessly, to keep away from his hens. Then the woodpigeons begin their incessant complaint, and there is one, so it sounds like, sitting on the bedroom chimney.

By this time, everything else is staking out their territorial claim, and it's light enough for the jackdaws to get going. Much as I love them, if you are short of sleep you could wish they would not chatter and chack quite so much as they fly off from their roosts to wherever they are foraging. But they are sociable creatures, I suppose, and like talking. In the end, window shut and room getting stuffy, you give up trying to get back to sleep and go and make tea.

For many years, one joy of summer was not the dawn chorus – for that stops by late May – but the martins who nested over our bedroom window. They came back each year to the little cup of their nest, and some of least of their children came back to the homes they built next to Mum and Dad. They never quite stopped talking through the short nights of summer – a low muttering and chuntering, never enough to disturb, but enough to be companionable if I was wakeful. But then, one summer, they did not return, and none have been seen since in the village. Perhaps they all fell to some gun in Italy or Malta, useless as food and hardly a mark of much machismo. My friends. They even came not to mind me watching them from the window as they flew up to the nest inches above the lintel, with their beaks full of flies for the welcoming, excited beaks of their nestlings.

An old house like this holds many such memories. The useless house martin nests stayed glumly untenanted under the eaves for years, until the sparrows moved in and made their usual mess and mayhem.

———— •• ————

A walk soon after an April dawn often takes us up the hill to the wood, the young wood I have already mentioned several times. It took a long time to look like a wood. But it does now. The wild cherry is hung with Housman's snow in season, and the spindle tree flaunts its flashy colours between the sombre shade of the yews. Deer and badger share the evening. The canopy in summer is closing – in some places has closed completely – and the biodiversity has increased exponentially. It is a good place, a place we take a pride in, planted with love, tended with care, and jealously defended against critics (and there are more than a few). Dogs walking their humans in the early morning or later afternoon form a friendly community, putting up with the humans cheerfully complaining about the weather, whatever it is doing – 'we need a nice drop of rain', 'could do with drying up', 'far too warm for the time of year', 'damn cold for May', [delete as appropriate]. I do it myself. The yaffle may interrupt you with his manic laugh. And you can always lean on the fence of the field next to the wood, think what might have been had you been able to be the farmer you wanted, and talk to Ron's ruminating sheep. They do not say much, though.

We have been so lucky this spring, despite the anxiety and strains of the coronavirus epidemic. Some nights have been chilly, but we have had no hard frost – yet! it could still come, for I have known snow at the end of April – to wreck the fruit blossom. The plum blossom and the greengage blossom is pretty well over, and the fruit has set. Young cherries on the geans in the wood have set, little green spheroids as big as the nail on a child's little finger. And the apple blossom is in full glory. The trees in the garden, the Cox's especially, are covered in it, and the Russet, untypically, is not shy this year. My only worry is that where there used to be a constant buzz of a host of bees working their socks off, this year I can only see a handful.

On a golden late afternoon after working all day in our studies, my lady and I went out for our dose of Healthy Exercise and eventually ended up, again, in the wood. The sun was still high enough for the air to be balmy, though one could in the shade guess at the chill to come before tomorrow's dawn. There are patches where the trees are thickly spaced along the rides and it's not easy to get among them. There was a little trodden path, obviously made by animals, leading off the main ride, and some clearing of suckers from the wild cherries along the ride had made it accessible and inviting. We followed it into an area of the wood where I had not been since it was planted that wet November morning all those years ago. Suddenly the underwood opened out, and we found ourselves between four large apple trees, whose canopies touched, almost like people lovingly twining their fingers together, and they were iced in blossom and drowned us in their perfume. Never have I smelt so powerfully the subtle wonder of apple blossom. And come autumn, God willing, these will be trees whose bounty we will harvest, for not many people will know of them.

But someone does. By a neighbouring beech tree, straight and tall with growing from her earliest youth in a close planted stand, someone has built a shelter out of branches: a shelter with a ridge pole of a trimmed branch, and trimmed branches leaning up against it. Big enough to sleep in... a child's den? Is that a child's work? Or does someone come here silently, secretly, to be alone in the community of trees? I know one woman who used to come and sleep in this wood on a summer night, when it was much younger and had no canopy to prevent you watching the grave circling of the stars.

But she is long gone.

Secrets are to be kept. We left: but, with courtesy, will be back in due season.

———◦———

An idyll, almost in the strict sense of the term. This was a morning to be out really early: it is hard to sleep when the bright sun is sidling round the dark curtain, and the birds are making such a din in the tree outside the window. A heavy dew, for it went cool last night, after a day when chopping kindling for next winter, and setting up the bamboos to form a frame for the runner beans, almost made me shed my shirt. The water drops edging the leaves scatter like bright sparks as I walk through them: I was wise to slip on gumboots, for there is no quicker way to get leather boots thoroughly soaked than to walk through wet grass. The sedge leaves by the river have an edging of dew which catches and refracts the light of the low sun into succeeding momentary glories of colour as I walk along the bank. The first swallows are already flickering along just above the water. The air is utterly still. There is no noise of distant traffic. There is not a single contrail in the sky.

The metal kissing gate into the meadow is cold, its noisy latch wet to the touch as I lift it. A thin mist rests just above the ground in the lower patches, dissipating as the sun gets up, almost while I watch. The cattle, some knee-deep in that indistinctness, are about their thoughtful business, and don't mind me walking among them. There is one under the first willow tree, reaching up to the thin ends of the drooping branches which are just showing their new leaves. I can hear her crunching them, and then she roughly yanks the branch down to get another good mouthful. They like that sort of thing: Ernie's milking cows, years ago when they used to walk up the lane past the garden from this very field, used to make a beeline for the leaves on the elm – Virgil's *Georgics*, indeed, recommends elm leaves as fodder for cattle. But willow has an added attraction: it is rich in aspirin, and tea made from the bark was an old country remedy for colds and headache. Our hens, too, used to jump up to grab the leaves of the weeping willow that shaded their run. I assume they had little headaches.

The path follows the raised river bank, passing the occasional hawthorn, just about to burst into its froth of heady, scented blossom. A brindled cow is standing by the water, her forelegs in the sedges, drinking, the water in the long distance down the straight river hazed in the last of the mist: a scene straight out of a painting by Albert Cuyp. A little further, and a well-grown bullcalf – aren't you getting too big for this now, dear boy? – noisily suckles his mother. My friend the nice old Hereford bull is a few yards away (is this calf his son? But the calf lacks the distinctive Hereford white blaze) grazing, and can't be bothered with me. Besides, his feet hurt, I think, and he always seems to find even slow walking just too much effort. By the cake of salt for their lick, two calves who have his white Hereford face lick on the salt raspingly.

By the big willow clump, a heron stands stock still, alert. He is poised for the quick stab down with that formidable beak: a mouse, perhaps, or a frog. But he is a shy bird, and seeing me opens his great slow wings and picks up his feet and glides a further hundred yards down the field.

The willow clump was once a tree, that once was a mere fence post driven in with a sledgehammer one January, that took root, and then grew into a tree that was split by a gale, so that half fell to the ground, which took root, which grew into a tree that then was split by a gale, and fell to the ground, and took root… the clump is a grateful shade for the cattle and the sheep when they are in here after haysel, and into the dog days of August when Sirius rises. The ground is trodden bare beneath it, the bark of the trees rubbed smooth and shiny in places where the sheep and cattle have rubbed themselves on it. Bits of wool have caught on the roughness of twig and bark.

By the pond – actually, an old coprolite pit, a relic of the time when mining those phosphatic nodules for fertiliser trebled the population of this village – where we scattered Hector the Labrador's ashes, a roebuck stands. 'And who are you?' his stare seems to say. For a minute, perhaps, we look at each other, immobile. Then he bounds off, but before he turns the corner, he stops, and looks back at me. Then off again.

Time for work: better get back. The climbing sun has burned off the last of the mist, and in this clear air you can see – well, it seems for ever. A couple of friendly dogs met me on the drove, their owners responsibly social distancing – a first reminder this morning of the shadow of the coronavirus, and the darker shadow of how our society is reacting to it. But let that pass, for now... My neighbour Luke is standing on the bridge as I turn into the lane, with his five-year-old son George. He has just seen the large grass snake – he is quite a regular – swimming along the river, and has got a photo of him. Young George is very excited because he has found a fossil. I ask him if he is really interested in fossils, and he says he is and one day he is going *definitely* to find a dinosaur. I can't do him a dinosaur, but I slip inside the house, and give him a belemnite and a little ammonite from my own cabinet of finds. But I can't put them in his eager hands: I have to put them on the ground in the lane.

And now, breakfast and prayers with my beloved, and fresh coffee.

Heaven does not get much better than this.

———•———

Our village Fair, which dates back to the time of King John, but is almost certainly older, was once one of the biggest events in the East Anglian mercantile calendar. It was the spring emporium, beside a navigable river, balancing the huge later summer one of Stourbridge, to which people came from all over Europe. It's inevitably now lost its commercial *raison d'etre*, but it is still a joyful day – if it does not pour down – for hundreds of people from a long way roundabout.

It opens with a proclamation – as most big mediaeval fairs did – of a Court of Pie Powder. (Summary justice, and settlement of trade disputes: a nice little earner for those who held the right of market.) The National Anthem is played: and then the children from the Primary School dance round the portable maypole, and their mothers shed a happy tear… and the fair is open.

The witness of those who hate things is often revealing. The Elizabethan and Jacobean radical preachers – it is too easy to call them 'Puritan', for there were many Puritans who, despite living a godly, righteous, and sober life, were full of charity, compassion, humanity and humility – hated many things, not least the yearly May festivals when people had a ball, got drunk, fornicated and what not. ('Go and see what Tommy is doing and tell him to stop it…'– there are too many people, religious or not, in all ages, who want to control people. They would have hated our fair, even though it is not riotous.) This disapproval did not start with those about whom Shakespeare and Jonson are so rude. One thing they really got steamed up about was May Day, when (like pre-Reformation Shrove Tuesday, or *mardi gras*,) people took the brakes off. Many would go off 'a-maying.' Robert Herrick's lovely May poem captures something of the

excitement of the rising at dawn to go off into the fields
and woods:

> *…There's not a budding Boy, or Girle, this day,*
> *But is got up, and gone to bring in May.*
> *A deale of Youth, ere this, is come*
> *Back, and with White-thorn laden home.*
> *Some have dispatcht their Cakes and Creame,*
> *Before that we have left to dreame:*
> *And some have wept, and woo'd, and plighted Troth,*
> *And chose their Priest, ere we can cast off sloth:*
> *Many a green-gown has been given;*
> *Many a kisse, both odde and even:*
> *Many a glance too has been sent*
> *From out the eye, Loves Firmament:*
> *Many a jest told of the Keyes betraying*
> *This night, and Locks pickt, yet w'are not a Maying.*
> *Come, let us goe, while we are in our prime;*
> *And take the harmlesse follie of the time.*
> *We shall grow old apace, and die*
> *Before we know our liberty.*
> *Our life is short; and our dayes run*
> *As fast away as do's the Sunne:*
> *And as a vapour, or a drop of raine*
> *Once lost, can ne'r be found againe:*
> *So when or you or I are made*
> *A fable, song, or fleeting shade;*
> *All love, all liking, all delight*
> *Lies drown'd with us in endlesse night.*
> *Then while time serves, and we are but decaying;*
> *Come, my Corinna, come, let's goe a Maying.*

Maypoles, which nearly every village had, were symbols of just what they hated. Each May morning it was the custom to deck these poles with wreaths of spring flowers, round which the people danced in a ring – which is what 'carol' originally meant – pretty nearly the whole day. London had some spectacular ones. For the church of St Andrew Undershaft got its name because each May for beyond the memory of man a maypole was set up opposite. Chaucer mentions it. But in 1527 a student mob stopped it. Would we now call it a 'd*eo*monstration'? They were full of ideas of Reform(ation) – though the word was not yet born – and, like enthusiastic and very young students everywhere, may well not have understood them very well. (If you see a parallel with political correctness or being 'woke' nowadays, well, that is up to you. But thank God young folk do get excited about ideas.) The ancient maypole – it was stored under the eaves of the church – survived until 1547 when another mob destroyed it utterly as a 'pagan idol'. Then there was the one that used to stand by Mary-le-Strand. This the later 'Puritans' called a 'last remnant of vile heathenism, round which people in holiday times used to dance.' In 1644 an ordinance of the dour Long Parliament swept all maypoles away, including this famous one, which, according to old Stow in his *Survey of London* (1598), stood 100 feet high. But when in 1660 the King came into his own again, a new, even taller one was set up amid much rejoicing. A contemporary pamphlet, *The Citie's Loyaltie Displayed*, says it was 134 feet high, and was erected

'upon the cost of the parishioners there adjacent, and the gracious consent of his sacred Majesty, with the illustrious Prince, the Duke of York. This tree was a most choice and

remarkable piece; 'twas made below [London] bridge and brought in two parts up to Scotland Yard, near the King's palace, and from thence it was conveyed, April 14, 1661, to the Strand, to be erected. It was brought with a streamer flourishing before it, drums beating all the way, and other sorts of musick. It was supposed to be so long that landsmen could not possibly raise it. Prince James, Duke of York, Lord High Admiral of England, commanded twelve seamen off aboard ship to come and officiate the business; whereupon they came, and brought their cables, pullies, and other tackling, and six great anchors. After these were brought three crowns, borne by three men bareheaded, and a streamer displaying all the way before them, drums beating and other musick playing, numerous multitudes of people thronging the streets, with great shouts and acclamations, all day long. The Maypole then being joined together and looped about with bands of iron, the crown and cane, with the king's arms richly gilded, was placed on the head of it; a large hoop, like a balcony, was about the middle of it. Then, amid sounds of trumpets and drums, and loud cheerings, and the shouts of the people, the Maypole, far more glorious, bigger, and higher than ever any one that stood before it, was raised upright, which highly did please the King's Grace and the illustrious Prince, Duke of York; and the little children did much rejoice, and ancient people did clap their hands, saying golden days began to appear.' A party of morris-dancer, 'finely decked with purple scarfs, in their half-shirts, with a tabor and a pipe, the ancient music… round about the Maypole.'

Well, are they phallic? Freud thought so, but then he thought that about many things. If your mind runs that way, so they are. Fanny Hill, in John Cleland's novel *Memoirs of a Woman of Pleasure* (1748), reverses the metaphor:

> *and now, disengag'd from the shirt, I saw, with wonder*
> *and surprise, what? not the play-thing of a boy, not*
> *the weapon of a man, but a maypole of so enormous a*
> *standard, that had proportions been observ'd, it must have*
> *belong'd to a young giant.*

On the other hand, sober scholars have proposed that it is a relic of the ancient Germanic and Nordic reverence for certain trees, and there certainly was such a reference once upon a time. But it all seems rather too serious and solemn for something which might have been, simply, fun.

Here is May in books forever;
May will part from Spenser never;
May's in Milton, May's in Prior,
May's in Chaucer, Thomson, Dyer;
May's in all the Italian books:—
She has old and modern nooks,
Where she sleeps with nymphs and elves,
In happy places they call shelves,
And will rise and dress your rooms
With a drapery thick with blooms.
Come, ye rains, then if ye will,
May's at home, and with me still;
But come rather, thou, good weather,
And find us in the fields together.

James Leigh Hunt

Everyone who grows vegetables knows all about the fear of a late frost, but we never learn: we always take a chance, trusting the fickleness of a few days of warm sunny weather, with a gentle westerly. All too often we get caught out, and you come down in the morning to the fresh leaves of the early spuds first whited, then shrivelled black with a frost. This year has been particularly hard: a warm – too warm – April, when for weeks the sunshine was unbroken and we began to talk of needing a nice drop of rain. But then the wind went round to the north, a dry quarter, and became a strong, searingly cold blast straight from Norway. Most evenings it died away, and the still air got colder and colder. We were prepared, and last thing before bed we were out there covering up anything that could suffer from frost with dustsheets – which, as we got away with it, gave us an enjoyable *Schadenfreude* when we saw others' misfortunes. But seeing the grey crispness on the lawn – well,

> *never-resting time leads summer on*
> *To hideous winter, and confounds him there;*
> *Sap checked with frost, and lusty leaves quite gone,*
> *Beauty o'er-snowed and bareness everywhere:*

A reminder, if we needed one.

Gerard Manley Hopkins' poem 'The May Magnificat' has many lovely lines, but these always come to mind when the exuberance all around you sets light to a joy inside you that demands – even if only through someone else's words:

> ...*Growth in every thing—*
> *Flesh and fleece, fur and feather,*
> *Grass and greenworld all together ;*
> *Star-eyed strawberry-breasted*
> *Throstle above her nested*
> *Cluster of bugle blue eggs thin*
> *Forms and warms the life within ;*
> *And bird and blossom swell*
> *In sod or sheath or shell.*
> *All things rising, all things sizing...*

The hawthorns are just about to overflow into their foam of blossom, a myriad heady-scented, black-stamened flowers each eyeing the sun and tinged with pink at the end of their ivory petals. So tempting to gather it and put it in flower arrangements, but when we first came to this part of England people urgently said, 'Don't you bring that old May into the house! That's an unlucky tree, that is.' A tree of ill-luck: they said the same of the elder: another unlucky tree, although of great beauty when its huge flat umbels spread to catch the sun. They say it was an on an elder that Judas hanged himself.

148

Summer

Sing, cuccu, nu. Sing, cuccu.
Sing, cuccu. Sing, cuccu, nu.

Sumer is i-cumin in—
Lhude sing, cuccu!
Groweth sed and bloweth med
And springth the wude nu.
Sing, cuccu!

Awe bleteth after lomb,
Lhouth after calve cu,
Bulluc sterteth, bucke verteth—
Murie sing, cuccu!
Cuccu, cuccu,
Wel singes thu, cuccu.
Ne swik thu naver nu.

Most folk associate this with 'An English Summer.' The *rota*, or round, (one of the oldest bits of English music to have survived from a time when English people were noted for their song and music, and a carol was a round dance sung to a tune like this) probably in fact relates to a longer period, starting in, say, late April. Indeed, the round has a repeated minor third, F-D, which is the call of the male cuckoo when first it arrives in late April, and the call's musical interval changes, as the season goes on, to a major third, then to a perfect fourth. (And then gives up.) The flowery mead sounds like late spring too, as do the lambs and calves. People seem to be unsure whether the 'bucke' is a billy goat or a deer, and whether it is farting or jumping about.

And then there is this lovely sonnet, which is certainly about the time when the nightingale, that lover of shrubby woodland margins and bushy hedges has arrived:

The soote season, that bud and blome furth bringes,
With grene hath clad the hill and eke the vale:
The nightingale with fethers new she singes:
The turtle to her make hath tolde her tale:
Somer is come, for euery spray nowe springes,
The hart hath hong his olde hed on the pale:
The buck in brake his winter cote he flinges:
The fishes flote with newe repaired scale:
The adder all her sloughe awaye she slinges:
The swift swalow pursueth the flyes smale:
The busy bee her honye now she minges:
Winter is worne that was the flowers bale:
And thus I see among these pleasant thinges
Eche care decayes, and yet my sorow springes.

Henry Howard, Earl of Surrey

Turtle doves are rare indeed now, and we have to put up with their cousins the woodpigeons and their doubtful sexual behaviour. But Howard knew, lived, the signs of early summer, the roebuck casting its winter coat, the hart rubbing off the velvet of his new horns against the paling of the deer park, the sloughed-off snake skins like the patterned papery ones I sometimes find. After all, the countryside and town were hardly very distinct then, and even a big town like London, far bigger than any other in England, had no more than about 50,000 people. Even much later, in little Cambridge, a hunted stag ran into St John's College and was killed. Carved on the underside of the lintel of G staircase in First Court is engraved 'Stag, Nov. 15, 1777'. That is a sharp reminder of how then (and for a good time afterwards) the fields lapped up against the little towns of England. Deer – the John's stag would have been a red deer – would indeed be a common enough sight if you set off to ride to London. Charles Darwin of Christ's College rode to hounds across the Cambridgeshire countryside, as did many undergraduates and graduates until only a short time ago, and Henry Gunning shot snipe and pheasant within a quarter of a mile of Great St Mary's Church.

But that last line: why does beauty and hope and joy, often make us, unaccountably, sad? Is it 'if spring comes, can winter be far behind?'

Howard, as it happens, was the last person to be beheaded by that murderous monarch, Henry VIII.

This morning, out early because the emphatic thrush on the tree outside the bedroom window was so loud that further sleep was impossible. I was in no hurry. It was a long time before I had to be back to pick up the chores of the day, like trying to talk to students about things they were supposed to have studied but, as is the way of the species, had 'looked at a bit.' My route, one of the usual ones, takes me along the stream, and past John's farm, then across the bridge and up the hill to the wood. It was a morning for dawdling, and looking, and stopping to smell things. The clear air was tranquil, the sun still not hot, the dew enough to wet my boots. Good to be alive and awake. As I passed the farm I heard behind me a very loud 'Cuckoo!', and then another, and then on my right (my good ear side), close, a cuckoo flew. And it then perched on the yew tree in John's garden. You don't often get a clear sight of them, heavily built birds, far too big you would think to sit on a dunnock's nest to lay its egg – in fact, I have only seen a few in my whole life. It called again, and again, while I stood still. It's only the male who calls, and that seems somehow appropriate, given its traditional association with cuckoldry. But birds take no heed of that. In a very few weeks its call will change to a single 'cuck' – which gives it its northern name, gowk.

The looked-for swifts, my ever welcome birds of summer, came back last week – they usually arrive around May 6th, just as they usually go on or about August 6th, and there seem to be more this year than in the last few years. They are lazily – well, it *looks* effortless – hawking along the hedge by the stream, feeding on the plankton of the air. The sickle wings slice the sky, and their steep turns, wings motionless, never fail to exhilarate. It lifts the heart, to see their swoop and sheer and elegance. They used to nest under the pantiles of the house opposite, and would fly in at speed straight into the little gaps, straight onto their nests. Something perfect. But alas, so few modern buildings give birds and our unregarded fellow creatures places to lay their young.

In the field by the lane leading up the hill, Michael has cut his hay – he must have done it yesterday, when the afternoon sun was as hot as it has been so far this year. The long stalks lie where the cutter bar has laid them, neatly parallel At the roots, the stems' green is nearer light tan for lack of the sunlight the uncut grass hid, and small creatures forage. A thrush flies from the hedge, picks a tiny Roman snail, not as big as the nail on your little finger, off a stem where it had glued itself to sit out this dry weather. The sun, still low, puts a sheen on the cut stems. And later, if this weather holds, perhaps tomorrow, the hay will be tedded, and set up into sweet smelling windrows to cure. And that smell on the wind always makes me think of Milton's lovely lines about

> *... one who long in populous City pent,*
> *Where Houses thick and Sewers annoy the Aire,*
> *Forth issuing on a Summers Morn to breathe*
> *Among the pleasant Villages and Farmes*
> *Adjoynd, from each thing met conceaves delight,*
> *The smell of Grain, or tedded Grass, or Kine,*
> *Or Dairie, each rural sight, each rural sound;*
> *If chance with Nymphlike step fair Virgin pass,*
> *What pleasing seemd, for her now pleases more,*
> *She most, and in her look summs all Delight.*

Milton, Paradise Lost (1676), IX 445ff

(I used to try to explain to the nowadays mainly urban young I taught just what hay's soft spiciness and the sharper notes of cattle smelt like. No chance. They got the bit about the fair virgin though.) Nobody is yet about. There are no human footmarks in the dew on the path into the wood save my own reaching out behind me. A muntjac deer looks up in surprise as I come round the corner of the hedge, and does not bother to run, just holds my glance for a few seconds, then merely skulks into the cover of the trees. Guelder roses are just coming into bloom – you can smell the sweet scent from their flat disks of dowdy fertile flowers, flamboyantly ringed by a large chalk-white ring of five-lobed sterile flowers. The dowdy ones in autumn will glory in red shiny berries. Dogwoods have hidden their bright red winter stems in dark green leaves, and their clusters of white flowers smell like the hawthorn blossom that has almost finished its frothy glamour for this year.

I can't resist going deep into the wood, off the ride, beneath the canopy of the young beeches – a secret place I try not to disturb too often, for it has its own life to get on with and I always feel a bit of an intruder. Over the dry brown leaves of yesteryear the trees stretch out horizontal planes of green to catch the light they need to make their nourishment. In a shaft of sunlight I catch a momentary magic of hoverflies, always welcome. The youthful sharp green of the new leaves is dulling now into the workaday of summer, like the bloom going off a new peach. The shade beneath them is thickening now, and the little seedlings that have germinated this spring will die off. I ought to have dug up a few of them some weeks back, and given them a new home. One more thing that did not get done...

The sun is hot as I come out of the green shade and turn for home. Basking on a large anthill at the side of the ride, a lizard. Bask on. He does not have to talk to students, or worry about their exams.

———◆———

Goldfinches nest later in the season than most small birds. They hatch their first brood around June and there will be some hatch even in September. It makes sense to nest late: the birth of their young coincides with times when food is plentiful. In early summer they will eat seeds of small plants like dandelions and groundsel, but come late summer and they gorge on the tiny seeds of thistles and teasels. Their Old English name is *Thisteltuige*, 'thistle-tweaker': their long, slim beaks are specialised tools for that. When they flock in autumn, it's always a minor joy as they lift off together, flashing gold and scarlet, from the patches of thistles in full downy seeding in patches of neglected ground. (But what does 'neglected' mean?)

Yet their flash of delighting scarlet and gold has sombre notes. Our ancestors never saw anything without its symbolic meaning. The ancient legend had it that when Christ was carrying the cross to Calvary a small bird – sometimes a goldfinch, sometimes a robin – flew down and plucked one of the thorns from the crown around His head. Some of Christ's blood splashed the bird as it drew the thorn out – an act of mercy echoed in the goldfinch's braving of the miniature thorns of the thistles. That is why, O Best Beloved, to this day goldfinches and robins have red on their plumage. So the goldfinch might be read as in so many paintings of the Madonna and Child, *Il Cardellino* prefigures the Passion: in 1506 Raphael painted John the Baptist offering the bird to the infant Christ.

I found a disused nest once. It was a deep cup of grass and mud, camouflaged with lichen which the owners must have gathered from the trees, lined with bits of black hair from the dog – his black hair was distinctive. I always chuck the combings on the lawn, as small birds can use them. I love seeing sparrows with great bristling black moustaches, and the hair is excellent insulation. Sign of the times though: in with the hair were strands of orange, shredded from old plastic baler twine. Which does not rot. Once I would not have given that a second thought, but now this reminder of what we have done to our planet shadows the sunlight of this spring.

A pair of longtailed tits tirelessly works up and down the birch tree picking off aphids feeding on the sap in the new leaves that are just breaking out.

———•———

Whitsunday morning, and grumpy. It is bone dry. No rain for six weeks – an extraordinary spring. Hot. Elderflowers, my Nemesis every year, broadcast their pollen far and wide, making a lethal cocktail with the grass pollen. Sneezes and snuffles, sweat. Impossible to sleep… Get up, walk around, try reading something calming, like the *Oxford Book of Mediaeval Latin Verse*. No good.

…But I am asleep, at last. At 0541 the phone rings. I get up and, very cross, pick it up to answer it, prepared to give them a piece of my mind. Nobody there. The number is a Brooklyn, NY, number, and I know nobody in that neck of the woods. (I check later on the Web and find that lots of folk have had calls from that number in the early hours.) Lie down, try to sleep. Impossible. Sneeze and snuffle. Blow nose. Now have sore sinuses. And now the wood pigeons, my un-favourite birds who feast on my carefully nurtured vegetables and never stop their tedious reiteration of 'My *Toe* hurts, Betty', have started their morning reporting of that discomfort to all those who cannot choose but hear. Like me. Not all at quite the same pitch or isochronously... I try to meditate, but keep coming back from High Thoughts to pigeons, and suitable, slow, ways to cook them. But I must have dozed off, for the next thing I hear (almost, it seems, in my ear) is 'MY *TOE* HURTS, BETTY'. Swearing, I leap up, and go to the open window, and on the sill, looking straight at me, is a woodpigeon with a vacant expression on its face. I am *not* Betty.

Give up. Rosanna, who also has had a bad night, suggests morning tea in the garden, where we can hear the pigeons and the collared doves and all the other feathered friends chorusing in their morning racket...I nearly drop asleep in the deckchair. But then Her restless Ladyship decides she will do the watering and the hose slithers over my bare feet... She calls to me that the pigeons have started eating the new plants of spinach. Her tee shirt has the legend, repeated in an endless chain, 'Today's today and I am glad it's today.' Someone said that to her, once.

Love and Charity on a fine Whitsunday morning. One does try. Doves are not, after all, pigeons.

PS: more out of desperation than anything, I cut out of semi-stiff damp-proofing black plastic a shape which reminds me (at least) of a hovering kestrel, tail spread, wings fluttering, fixed it to a right-angled length of wire which then drops into a hole at the end of a long metal tube. I lashed that onto a post among the vegetables, and my creation swivels and flutters high over them. And so far, for hours no pigeons have been seen near the veg. Visitors will be told that it is a piece of kinetic sculpture.

———•◦•———

And talking of predators... How the world has changed for the better in some ways. When we first came to Reach a kestrel was a rare sight: they had suffered the fate of so many raptors at the top of the food chain, with pesticides accumulating in their systems to the point where their breeding was a problem, with either infertile eggs or eggs so thinshelled they could not be incubated. However, this last week the village magazine carried this wonderful story...

A neighbour keeps her horses in a field near the wood. In late April she found a seemingly dead kestrel there. She took it home with her, just in case, and as she put it in a cat box it moved, crawled, but could not stand. She offered food and water, then took it to the local vet who could not help, but they called the Raptor Foundation. They sent someone over to collect the bird. They removed a massive tick, but, as the kestrel got weaker, they then drove 70 miles to specialists in Leicester for an X-ray, which showed a tiny metal fragment in its innards. Back in the Raptor Foundation aviary, the bird slowly recovered over 3 weeks, and the metal passed through its system. Then they brought it back to where it was found, released it, and it flew strongly into the wood. This would simply not have happened a generation ago. I remember a kestrel I myself found on a walk down the fen, unable to fly, reeling on the ground. It had not the energy to protest when I picked it up, though those great eyes glared. And as I held it, the light died in them and its body became limp. There was no mark on it. But I could smell the poisons the local farmer – a nice chap, as it happened – was at that very moment spraying on his nearby field.

———●——

Breeding everywhere you look: the first apples setting, flowers busy and noisy with fertilising bees and insects, and nodding with the tiny weight. On the stream two moorhen mothers try to keep their (second?) broods of tiny black fluffy chicks, not as big as hen's eggs, out of mischief and danger. They are, after all, just bite size for a lurking pickerel, and there is often one waiting immobile at the end of the garden. Moorhens rarely bring off more than a couple of their brood. Nature is prodigal of life. My friendly cock blackbird – I recognize him from last year by a tiny white feather on his right cheek – is even more friendly, after some months of relatively indifferent politeness, as he busies himself all day finding food for his nestlings. He likes me hoeing the vegetable garden, which is not always convenient, for sometimes I have got a good rhythm going and he skips out of the way of the blade only just in time. There is a sense of urgency, almost haste. Sometimes you find a half-fledged bird dead at the foot of the hedge, where it has fallen out of the nest – or been pushed. The woodpigeons are incessantly and noisily copulating on rooftops and unsuitably unsteady branches, even on phone wires – and, just now, even just below the thrush at the top of the big sycamore who is loudly singing his 'I am here! Keep off!' song. One sees why pigeons are now as common as muck, the commonest British birds. In fact, I had never met woodpigeons before I came south, and I find them very difficult to like (except cooked) if you are at all involved in vegetables or any sort of eatable crop. They are flying compost heaps. They are noisy. They never stop. They make a fearful clatter with their wings as they take off – so much so that in some parts they call them 'clatter doves'. Their large chest muscles – their redeeming culinary feature – power an explosive take-off and as they can't fly through small gaps, they don't even try, but simply clatter through the leaves and branches making a din. (Those wing muscles... I once clocked a pigeon flying along beside the car at 65 mph.) Some mornings I come down and there, half a dozen of their portly forms are waddling across the lawn. More often you see them in threes: two male and a female, as if a *ménage à trois* is in prospect. For they never stop courting, the male circling round the female – being rude to the rival – then bowing, spreading his tail, while she just looks unconcerned and if possible carries on guzzling. After all, she lays three clutches a year, and a girl does need her food. (Their breeding makes rabbits look continent.) Sometimes he tries to impress her by flexing the three parallel white bars on his neck – at a distance they look like one – but I cannot imagine flattering oeillades and most speaking looks in those *eau de Nil* eyes in that little head. But he does know the way to a girl's heart, for prior to getting together seriously he will feed her tasty bits from my garden... Actually, they feed their young on what the village folk told a young me, who thought he was having his leg pulled, on pigeon's milk. It's actually a regurgitated broth of vegetables and invertebrates.

In the end, she will show some interest, and the two will twine their necks together for a few minutes in what looks like the play of lovebirds. But that is being anthropomorphic.

Pigeons and their very public courtship get me thinking about other creatures, and about humans. Even our recent ancestors had very little privacy; and they were very lucky if they brought up all their brood to adulthood. Houses, cottages, were tiny by our standards. This house, once two two-up-two-down cottages, has small rooms, and I know that less than a century ago a couple not only brought up seven children in one half but also shared it with two of their grown-up sons. So what about intimacy, love-making and all the rest of it?

The easy season, when you could virtually live outside, is, I am sure, the answer. A spring walk in the dusk, a summer hayfield, a May morning in the woods and fields, a languorous evening by the hedge at the edge of a new mown harvest field, and who knows what might happen? 'Walking out with So and So', might be close to the mark. And looking at humans as objectively as one can, being one, as animals with a breeding cycle, does stress the survival advantage of outdoor courtship. Conception between, say, a drying and warming May, when much of the spring sowing and hard work on the land has been done, and a golden mellow September means births between February and June, when times are getting easier, the weather is warmer and healthier, and food is getting more plentiful after the rigours of winter. It is even more relevant to a hunter gatherer society, as which we evolved.[2] I have never had time really to test this theory on a large enough sample, but snapshot searching of country parish registers does seem to support this, with the majority of baptisms in the summer months. It might even be that the literary, clichéd, association of spring with love is a record of the actuality. Nightingales, the bird of love, don't start to sing here till May...

———•—————

Nightingales used to sing decades ago down in the unkempt bits of the Fen, and then they disappeared. But they are now, sometimes, back, singing in the little trees of the wood to the silent stars, and one wonderful June we could hear Philomela bewail her plight from dusk to dawn through the open window of our bedroom. The wood and its open patches, where dieback has taken its toll of the young ash trees, have brought back the blue butterflies, and the moths, and a host of little creatures have moved in whom one catches in the corner of the eye, sometimes, while walking with the busy dog. There are still golden moments. My grandson and I went up with the dog one June gloaming to hear the nightingales, which he had never heard, and through the gloom we glimpsed another lad, about Tom's age, and his father the shepherd

---

[2] See the intriguing remarks on hunter-gatherer fertility in James C. Scott, *Against the Grain: a Deep History of the Earliest States* (New Haven and London: Yale University Press, 2017) pp.113-5.

(he is a teacher really, but what is the difference?) making their way up the dark lane towards us. Courtesies, and chat, and then companionable silence, as we waited for the show to begin in the bushes below the big old ash tree that has been there a century. But then came the noise of an engine, and along the hilltop track in his unlit Jeep slowly comes young Mike, who once had a tame jackdaw, and used to play with my son. His son is beside him and the rifle with which they have been rabbiting is along the dashboard. More chat and pleasantries... and not a nightingale to be heard. But Gareth takes out his mobile phone, into which he has programmed many bird's songs, and plays the song of a nightingale...And all Heaven breaks loose as every nightingale for acres around joins in. Tom will remember the song of the nightingale, and a golden evening.

One woman I know very well indeed (as far as anyone can know the secrecy at another's heart) goes forest bathing when she can, usually first thing in the morning. This old Japanese practice, *shinrin yoku*, is a search for quiet of mind, fullness of sense, grounding in that universal life of which we are a part. It sounds very New Agey, but Wordsworth and Thoreau, John Muir and Ralph Waldo Emerson – and Martin Heidegger and Richard Rohr – would know exactly what it was about. Go off the paths, be alone in among the trees – even our teenage wood will do very well – where little, narrow, trodden paths show where badger and fox, deer and rabbit, travel on their mysterious occasions. You're your own Walden. Stop. Be still. Listen. This friendly trunk is ideal to rest your back against. Be calm, quiet amongst the trees, yet with senses alert to smells, the smell of leaf mould and bark, and blossom, and decay; sense the flaws of wind, and how leaf and branch play the changing light; be alert to texture of bark and leaf, hearing the tiny noise a leaf makes as it falls. Time will fly… but what *is* time?

Wordsworth put the case well, responding to his sceptical friend Matthew – perhaps based on the man who taught him, and taught him well, at Hawkshead school:

'The eye – it cannot choose but see;
We cannot bid the ear be still;
Our bodies feel, where'er they be,
Against or with our will.

'Nor less I deem that there are Powers
Which of themselves our minds impress;
That we can feed this mind of ours
In a wise passiveness.

'Think you, 'mid all this mighty sum
Of things for ever speaking,
That nothing of itself will come,
But we must still be seeking?

'Then ask not wherefore, here, alone,
Conversing as I may,
I sit upon this old grey stone,
And dream my time away.'…
One impulse from a vernal wood
May teach you more of man,
Of moral evil and of good,
Than all the sages can.

The wood does not have to be vernal. Any season will do.

It is nearly June, after a year dominated by 'now you can, now you can't' Covid lockdowns, and there is a feeling of things pent up everywhere – by a long cold April, by a torrentially wet, cold May, by the sense of missing so much. All that cheerful easiness, friendliness, in a lovely spring that in this village made Lockdown 1 of 2020 feel almost like the sort of re-calibrating holiday of which one dreams seems not quite there, as if overtaken by a sort of impatience. Even the trees and plants seem pent up, for here we are, four weeks before the sun turns back from the Tropic, and the oaks and ashes are not in full leaf.

But at last, the day before yesterday, the locks seem loosed. The wind has gone southerly. It is warm. Suddenly, it is summer even if the surprised ashes and oaks have got a lot of leafing to do. The Queen Anne's Lace is suddenly a froth of delicate white at roadsides. All at once, people seem to be smiling more. The young are making sure everyone knows they have bodies. People are saying, 'Aren't we lucky with this weather?'

I know my new neighbour Luke, who loves country things, wants to keep bees, and I encouraged him a long time ago, and offered him the hives I have never got rid of. But despite trying, he can't get a nucleus of bees for love or money from any of the dealers till next year or even the year after that. 'There are no bees', they tell him. So I have told him he can set up a decoy hive behind my greenhouse – his garden is too small for hives with two dogs and two small children – but, shaking my head – (hang on, this is what Colin was like!), warn him that he may not get any local swarms – and, anyway, 'no use after June... you know the saying, "Swarm in May, worth a load of hay, swarm in June, worth a silver spoon, swarm in July, not worth a fly"'.

And now May is nearly over, and no honeybees about, to speak of. I am once more doing my pessimism act to Luke over the garden wall, when Steve the archaeologist comes paddling up the river in his canoe, with news of a swarm on the river bank in a hawthorn blooming in full glory. So off we go, with my old bee box with 'LIVE BEES' in red on the lid: Colin gave me it after I had gone to Cambridge Station Parcels Office to collect a new colony of bees that had arrived by train for him. The swarm is at a convenient height, but our footing is a bit precarious, right on the edge of the water – after all, bees do not swarm so as to make things easy for us. We knock the football-sized lump of bees into the box, immediately turn it upside down on the ground (leaving a small gap for ingress and egress), and leave them for an hour or two to settle – and to ensure we have got Her Majesty.

We went back that evening, fearing we might have lost her and her court, for it is twenty years since I took a swarm and I am out of practice. But we have indeed got her. In the slanting golden light across the Fen, we carried the box carefully along the uneven drove back to the garden. Then, one of the most joyful sights of a summer evening: Luke holds the box over the white sheet I have spread in front of the entrance to the hive, and shakes the mass of *his* bees onto it. There is an explosion of noise, the air is full of agitated bees, but they are mostly in the amorphous mass the colour of Christmas pudding that lies heaving on the sheet. Then comes that magical moment when the scouts somehow tell the queen that there is a Des. Res. to let nearby, and she runs up into the entrance and the whole mass within seconds is all facing in one direction, pressing forward, crawling over each other in their eagerness, rushing up the slope to join their sovereign in the warm dark of the hive. To see that is one of the greatest country pleasures I know. Luke went to get young George, 7, and little Maisie, 5, in their nightclothes to come and see. They will remember that. (Next morning they come round to ask if the honey was ready.)

In the soft dusk the hive snores gently, about A flat, and in the low north-eastern sun of dawn the flowering bushes are alive with busy ladies who will live a few weeks and then die, their duty done, to be replaced by others the queen is laying in the hive. The garden feels alive again. I had not realised how much I had missed my bees. My Lady said, 'I have not seen you so animated for weeks!' Today brought back, sharp as a pin, all those other hivings, the ones that worked and the ones that didn't, those years of companionable working with Colin, and then with my son, as despite us the bees carried on, wild creatures whose life and purpose for a short time marched with ours. You do not tame bees.

There is a tailpiece. That was two nights ago. The next morning, bright, already hot, I was writing in the study with door open and someone called me. It was my neighbour Christina, from Brazil, dressed for the weather. Breathlessly, in her emphatic way, she says, 'Charles, we have a *BIG* swarm up in one of our trees… can you lend us a hive?' 'How are you going to take it?' 'I shall go up the ladder and put them into a box or cut the branch off and carry it down.' (They are, as it happens, 20 feet up.) She must have seen me looking with some disbelief at her skimpy shorts and low tank top, for she says, reassuringly, 'I shall put my suit on.' I give her the hive and wait developments…

I take my hat off to that lady. Up the ladder once, bring the bees down, and failure. You don't tame bees. They tolerate you, but are busy with their own world, which is not ours, just overlaps with it. The queen is still stolidly up there and all the bees go back to where they were, as indeed they should. But so does Christina with grim determination and a saw. This time she cuts off the branch, and carries it down the steep and none too steady, ladder with a huge blob of bees hanging on to it. And hives them successfully, near her newly planted vines. Not a single sting.

But two good swarms in two days... The poor things must have been desperate for the weather to turn. But it has done, and soon the limes will be dripping their sweetness and the bees will be busy from dawn to dusk. I'd love to think a hive could, in its own measure, feel joy. It is good to have them in the garden again.

———◆———

In a little open patch in the wood, all of a sudden one June the ground was dotted with bee orchids, not the commonest of flowers. And they do look like bees perched on the greyish green of the plants – so much so, indeed, that the Wildlife Trust website tells me that it is 'a sneaky mimic – the flower's velvety lip looks like a female bee. Males fly in to try to mate with it and end up pollinating the flower. Sadly, the right [solitary] bee species [*Eucera Longicornis*] doesn't live here, so this orchid is self-pollinated in the UK.' The oldest people in the village took our surprise with some amusement, for they remembered them growing there long before the silent springs of the '50s and '60s. Perhaps they had been simply waiting… perhaps the animals wait, the land itself waits, until our brief hour is done. Just so, beneath the towns, beneath the brick and tarmac present, the fields like memory lie sleeping underneath.

———•———

May and June, as the year begins to luxuriate and the sparer, lithe beauty of spring begins to thicken into middle age, show up so many things you left undone, did not get cleared up, when things were quieter. There was a dead branch on an old plum tree that I ought to have trimmed off months ago, but I did not get round to it. Anyway, better late than never. So the other morning off it came, and I began to saw it up for the few logs it would make. But under the loose bark I stumbled on a touching domestic scene: a mother earwig with her brood.

Now, I have always liked earwigs even though they do do some damage to my growing vegetables. For earwigs are among the few non-social insects who look after their young. The mother will make sure her eggs are warm and safe, defending them with her formidable pincers, and she only leaves them to eat if the clutch has gone bad. She continuously cleans the eggs to protect them from fungi. She even helps the nymphs in hatching. The nymphs, when hatched, are almost transparent and scurry to nest under their mother, who protects them until their second moult, feeding them with regurgitated food and their own moulted skins. But, in an act of striking impiety, if she dies before they are ready to leave, the nymphs may eat her.

I left the branch for later: it could wait. Partly my problem is I have a conscience about things left undone, and about how hard the old folk worked on this land I call my own. (But they did not, so far as I know, write books too.) Over the years I have I have desultorily collected old (fashioned) books on country lore and husbandry. (You might have guessed as much.) An occasional dip into them, when on the supposedly purposeful way to another book, reminds how much easier things are for us, and how much *time* the old way of doing things took, how much detail had to be noticed. John Evelyn, for example, writing in *Directions for the Gardiner* [sic] *at Says-Court But Which May be of Use for Other Gardens* (never published in his lifetime) has this advice for June: he says you should sow lettuce, chervil and radishes for salad, and gather your herbs for drying – put them in the shade, not the sun, he says. That garden of the lovely house by the Thames took lots of work: 'Look to your *Bees* for swarms … and begin to destroy *Insects* with *Hoofs, Canes,* and tempting baits, &c, gather *Snails* after rain &c.' (The 'hoofs' were sheep's hooves upside down on sticks, as earwig traps. Nowadays organic gardening books recommend a plastic cup, upside down, stuffed with honey-soaked grass.) As snails have homing instincts, you either destroy them (which I always find hard, as I find them interesting and even beautiful) or take them a long way away… up to a mile, like house mice. The latter get back somewhat quicker. But time, time, time… and they are not making any more of it.

Sayes Court, by the way, was let out to Czar Peter (he who was later called the Great) when he was working as a shipwright, incognito, at Deptford dockyard. He wrecked Evelyn's beloved garden, having his men push him in his cups all over the lawns (no lawnmowers then – first patented in 1830 by a man called, delightfully for one who had such influence on gardeners, Budding) and the meticulous flowerbeds in a wheelbarrow. Parliament voted Evelyn a massive sum in compensation for the damage to his house and garden.

I wonder: do we speak of 'velvet lawns' in homage to the fact that Budding got the idea for his mower from a machine used to shear the nap of velvet?

———●———

The harsh talk of magpies in a thick, shrubby part of the wood told me something was going on, for when they make that noise to each other they are usually bent on mischief – or simply, from their perspective, dinner, and they often work in pairs. Sure enough: in their pauses I could hear a furious remonstration of smaller birds, and, then, one cry, shriek rather, that rapidly shrank, diminuendo, to silence. Dinner and death. It's all around.

In the hedges the dog roses – greatly underrated, hardly noticed, flowers, because they are common and just happen year after year – are beginning to drop their petals. Later there will be the large red hips which seem to offer such gustatory delight. A spectacular plant: yet my beloved showed me something I had overlooked all my life the other day. For each petal is heart shaped; and under a lens it shows the most delicate veining.

Later, the bushes will be covered with their spectacular scarlet fruit, which looks so tempting. But they have little flesh, and your mouth is full of the straw-coloured seeds. Moreover, don't even bother trying to make rose hip gin – you can steep most fruits in gin and get something decent. But this one looks like urine and tastes simply of Vitamin C. That richness in that vitamin in fact is why in the 1940s in this village children as young as five were paid 3d a gallon (5 litres!) to collect the hips, to be sent off to make Delrosa Rose Hip Syrup. I knew some of those children in their later years, and they did not look back on the scratchy, spiky task with pleasure.

But the birds love them, and when they feed on them there are splotches of their seed-filled droppings everywhere, with those seeds cleverly transported to a site where they can soon colonise.

Let's have a digression on cowpats. For in the field by the river the new cowpats Michael's cows have generously splotched are getting a crust like brown pastry on the top as the hot sun dries them out. When we were children, we used to pick them up when they got really dry, and throw them like Frisbees – on which, see below. But at the moment they are still liquid enough underneath to be useful soaked in a bucket of water for feed for the tomatoes and the courgettes. I am only doing what humans have done for at least 8,000 years. For essentially it is undigested, bacteria-packed plant residue, with valuable amounts of nitrogen, phosphate, potash and sulphur, which plants need.

Some facts – how helpful the internet can be sometimes! Your ordinary dairy cow dumps 15 tons a year, and a beef animal about 11. They are doing well, for a full-grown African elephant, weighing around eight times more than a cow, only manages 50 tons per year. And humans, well: a cow weighs some 10 times more than a man but the man produces just 1% of the weight of dung that the cow does. (Around 0.15 tons – 330 pounds or so – a year.)

And flies, and beetles... The female horn fly lives by sucking the cow's blood – but as the cow begins to defecate, she whizzes round the back and lays her eggs in the steaming stream of mid-air dung. They will hatch in the pat in large numbers and become pupae within a week. And then there are the flies most familiar, the whizzing ginger-hued *scathophagidae*, a traditional fly-fishing inspiration. Izaak Walton described the 'cow-dung-fly' lure in *The Compleat Angler* (1653) as 'the dubbing, light brown and yellow mixed: the wing, the dark grey feather of a mallard'.

But there's more than just flies in the world of a cowpat. Fly eggs and larvae attract insects who set about eating them. Other creatures come up from the soil: nematode worms and flukes, and several sorts of predatory beetle join the frenzy to find prey, and deposit eggs, and they tunnel close to the rainproof surface and help to oxygenate the upper layer. Some feed on the dung to get at the microbiotic content. Then along come digger wasps and ichneumons to seek grubs in which to lay eggs that hatch and eat their hosts alive. Spiders, woodlice, earwigs and earthworms move in underneath. But this menagerie does not have it all its own way. Beetles, especially dung beetles, dry out and break down the cowpat, rolling it up into little balls which they take to burrows as food for the grubs that will hatch from the eggs they lay in the balls. Doing that kills other pupae in the cowpat by depriving them of moisture. Moreover, fungi thrive in dung. One toadstool that grows in cowpats catapults its spores into the surrounding vegetation – a relatively safe space, as another ecological function of cowpats is deterring close grazing to ensure that some grass patches seed. Then there is the dung roundhead mushroom, probably the first ever material used to make blue pottery. You can also use dung to make bricks or – how wasteful! – as fuel. It actually burns hotter than wood, with no smell or soot. Its uses are endless, it seems… in medicine, some cultures use fresh dung to treat open wounds, and dung poultices were used in parts of Britain well into the 1800s. An 1841 leaflet says they were 'still used by the lower orders as a cataplasm for bruises and sprains, applied hot as the patient can bear'. Another told of a man in St George's Hospital in London whose ulcerous leg was due to be amputated until a nurse, schooled by her Yorkshire village grandmother, applied dung poultices – a hot 'cowsharn' – twice a day and forbade alcohol. In two weeks, the sores began to heal and the poor chap made a 'full recovery', desperate for a drink and never wanting to go near a byre again.

And finally, cowpats have their own sport. In the USA, dried cowpats are known as 'cow chips' – and bored farmers in the Mid-West (and heaven knows the flat Mid-West can be boring) use those chips for entertainment. Beaver, Oklahoma, hosts the annual World Cow Chip Throwing Contest, where the record is 188ft 6in. But we kids in Lancashire got there first, though we never made 188ft 6ins, even with a sea wind behind the throw.

Often, in mid-June, exams and much of the marking being over, we – later, I on my widowed own, and then, even later, with Rosanna Petra – would have my students come out for the day to the house in the country, for lunch, walks, talk, and more talk. By that time of year you could usually count on decent weather. It was always slightly uneasy, that meeting them off the bus: they were meeting me (and the dog) in a new, non-academic, role, and some found that at first difficult to handle. For my part, I was always concerned about practical things: what they would have on their feet and whether they would have had the sense to bring (hopefully unnecessary) waterproofs. For a walk was obligatory, and would not be on tarmac. Some were indeed properly shod and dressed. But over the years, it became more and more apparent that a growing number had, literally, never been to 'the country', had never been outside a town with pavements and street lights and so on, had never felt mud under their feet. Talk of the stars and constellations, the Hunting of Orion with his dog following, the Chair of Cassiopeia, and from most you got – get – blank looks.

People like my students are the lucky ones, though: they will have a certain freedom to choose their path. But their overwhelmingly urban-centred life is a symptom of something wrong with the way most of us live. As a species, we in the affluent countries have moved 'inside': we live in cars, in tiny rooms, in tower blocks, for much of the time in artificial light and with a half-perceived background of mechanical noise. For most of us, the predominating colours in our urban environment are grey, brown, black. Our feet walk on tarmac, on carpet, on tile. Our TVs may show us trees and fields and mountains and animals, but they are devoid of smell, or wind, or feeling, and you can be watching the grave courtship of the elephant seal or the intimacies of the midnight owl with the smell of cooking dinner in your nostrils and (perhaps) the pre-prandial drink in your hand. Someone else's camera chooses for you what to see – which is not the whole, not real time. Yet the evidence is increasingly stacking up that if you want mental health issues, this is the right way to go about it. For we are denying a fundamental part of our evolutionary nature: as Thoreau and all the others saw.

I hate the expressions 'Nature' or 'the natural world', for are we not ourselves part of it, integral? Never mind: 'Nature's' smells, sounds, geometry, texture are what conditioned the evolution of our brains. Our minds *need* the wild for us to be fully human animals. It has been shown by many studies that there is a persuasive circumstantial link between social and personal violence in deprived areas and the incidence, or not, of trees and green space. Several pieces of research have shown that recovery after surgery is faster when people can see trees and plants from the window of their convalescence. Trees are an important part of a supportive, humane environment. Perhaps we like them, and miss them when they are not there, because, deep in our subconscious, in our species' memory if you like, their shape offers refuge, shelter, and the bounty of food in due season. Show me the person who does not find intoxicating the smell of earth just before long awaited rain, and then newly wet. Our parasympathetic nervous system[3] is triggered when

---

[3] The parasympathetic is one of three divisions of the autonomic nervous system. Some call it the rest and digest system. It conserves energy for it slows the heart rate, increases intestinal and gland activity, and relaxes sphincter muscles in the gastrointestinal tract.

we are in 'nature'; some soil bacteria release chemicals that increase stress resilience.

A long digression, but one the ideas of which press on me more and more. We have taken the wrong path, and continuing will not get us to anywhere we want to be. We have to rethink… and often this subject came up with my students, relaxing over tea after their expected walk, which some enjoyed for the first time. They might well have talked to Ron's half-grown lambs or Andrew and Helen's little Dexter bull who, after a grand life, will become delicious meat. And more than a few had felt the same, but had not articulated it. It takes a lot of courage to break out of the trap where you feel comfortable. Some – I know some – come to love their captivity, and no longer look out of the window to see the stars, or long for the wind on their cheek. Send out for a pizza, forget the soils and air and water and life of which it has been made.

———•———

This is the time when – especially in a warm damp spell – weeding and grass cutting is relentless. Turn your back and the bright nets of chickweed and the rosettes of shepherd's purse, and the tremulous triangular leaves of fat hen (which hens really do like) are everywhere in the veg garden. Nettles are waist high by the hedge, the old mauve opium poppies (which once upon a time every cottage garden grew for winter agues and flus) are reaching to the light through the dark green of the rows of spuds, and my bête noire, the sly convolvulus, the twisty, twiny, giant white sort, which stinks when you cut it and its white sap bleeds, has begun to festoon the hollies and strangle plants in its way. That one I have always hated, the way it creeps up on you unseen and then is suddenly blanketing everything, flaunting its evasion of your watchfulness with its brilliant white trumpets – particularly huge the higher up and nearer the light they are. My children knew these flowers as 'Granny Pop out of Bed', and like other children in the village would say, 'Granny, granny, pop out of bed', squeeze the base of the flower head, and the flower would jump off. Soil stains are ineradicable in the cracks of your hardened fingers. Your back aches. But it has got to be done, for Old Thomas Tusser is firm: 'who weeding slacketh/Good husbandrie lacketh.' I can imagine him shaking his head if he had seen my garden when I had not touched it for a week.

———◆———

Dragonflies – the big ones, like *Aeschina cyanaea* or *Anax imperator* – are suddenly in evidence, like tiny helicopters in their clattering flight over the hot afternoon garden, when the sun is full on it. Hodge, our last cat, used to try to catch them, jumping up into the air, and occasionally managed it, and crunched them like barley sugar. Damsel flies, their close relatives, also abound. At tea in the garden with friends this week, a male *Calopteryx virgo* (rightly called the 'Beautiful Demoiselle', though a male can hardly be a demoiselle, exactly) settled on my plate, an inch and a half of brilliant beauty, a metallic blue body with dark blue wings. They are not uncommon, but their beauty is. Guests were duly appreciative.

My neighbour Joss, a fine painter, loves horses, and, despite her severe arthritis which made riding difficult, for years looked after an elderly garron pony whom she had known in Scotland, and who became a much loved village character. Her deep hollowed back, almost an armchair, and her solid bulk spoke of her working life – what garrons were bred for – of bringing deer off the hill after stalking. Then she died. Joss rescued two donkeys, both jennies, who had been badly treated, and nursed them back with her love and care to a sort of happiness. One seemed to be getting very fat, and the vet was called, and recommended a restriction on her fodder, but she continued to round. Joss called the vet back and insisted on a scan, which revealed that, all unbeknown, she was pregnant. Well, in due time this summer the little filly was born, all legs and unsteadiness for the first hour or so, then, after a bit of fumbling, found its dam's milk and tucked in, tail going nineteen to the dozen. It has had a good start to life, and I love to pass the field and see two sets of large ears and one of small pricked, and looking at me with curiosity. The little one has a ball to play with. Why do we assume that animals never play?

Some years ago I cut down a large sycamore in the garden, and split most of it up for logs. It's not a great firewood – it burns very fast – but I hate waste. One round of the trunk, however, I left, and used it for a time as a block on which to chop kindling. As the rains came and went over the seasons, it got more and more rotten, until finally a vigorous chopper stroke split it down the middle.

I pushed the halves to one side and rather forgot about them, as the wood lost more and more of its strength and got lighter and lighter.

Well, fits of tidiness in the garden do overtake me occasionally. It may well be the first spring sunshine that gets me going, as it gets most things thinking of – well, whatever. I decided some months ago to clear up the bit I call the glory hole, where I do things like chopping and sawing. So I moved one of the halves of the sycamore – it was very light, almost like balsa – and suddenly saw a pair of beautiful but distinctly surly eyes looking at me. It was a very fat grey toad, skin looking like a pachyderm's, clearly cross at being woken up too early. He/she slowly raised herself on her forearms, which from that angle are very like ours, and began a slow crawl away. 'Oh, I am so sorry, I did not mean to disturb,' I said, and gently replaced the rotten log, carefully putting a piece of wood under one end so that I did not crush someone else who lived in the garden I call mine, for the moment.

Now I like toads – in fact like them more than the more elegant frogs. I wish Philip Larkin had not been so rude about them, making them symbolise all that is unpleasant about hated work. I welcome them into the vegetable garden, where I have been gardening organically since before the word was common. I rely on them to eat up the nasties, as I rely on the hoverflies and ladybirds and lacewings in summer to gobble up aphids. So it is good news when you know you have resident toads, and sometimes you spot them looking thoughtfully out from under the strawberry leaves or on a sunny day finding a shady retreat beneath the chard. Always welcome.

In that wet spring when I had to break in a new allotment, on Ely's stiff and sticky clay, 'Cruel hard land,'

I thought, as I straightened up and saw against the sky the west tower of the Cathedral. The water had run down the slope and ponded into a pool about 3 feet square and about 3 inches deep at the bottom of my patch. Then my eye caught movement: and I saw eyes, and more eyes. But they were not concerned about me and my digging. The water was full of toads, mating, locked in their nuptial embrace with no regard to size and compatibility. It seemed to be a slow rather than passionate business, but who can tell what goes through a toad's mind? That seriously cheered up my mood, for if there were that many there, then clearly the ecosystem was in good heart, and the land might be productive after all. (It was, as it happens – mine were the best spuds on the allotments in the drought year that followed.)

But what I am leading up to was something extraordinary, magical, delightful. It was early summer, and as the sky softened into dusk I was writing in the study with the French door open because of the heat. Suddenly, my eye caught a movement near the sleeping Hector – a dog who cared for none of these things. It was a toadlet: not more than half an inch long, but still with the fine eyes of the family. I caught him in my hands, and felt his little limbs trying to escape the hot cavern of my grasp. I took him outside and put him beneath the frilly-edged leaves of alchemilla. But as I went back in, there he was – no he could not be – but there is another, and another, and another. Some were tiny, some about two inches long, all for some toady reason making their way into the house. It was the same in the kitchen, where we had left the door open. Now, clearly, privileged as we were to have so many visitors, this could not go on, for when they had eaten up our resident and useful spiders, and any passing slugs, what would they have lived on? So, looking unselfishly to their best interests, we shut the doors and scoured the house catching the toadlets, and putting them in a pan – they were not too pleased about being so close to each other – and then taking them outside. But on the dark terrace were even more... We tiptoed, in torchlight, through them, and put our charges down on the vegetable garden where they might grow into mighty slug-devouring toads and sleep, fat and happy, under a fallen log next winter.

Why am I writing this? Well, it seemed, somehow, a privilege to be so visited: a bounty of happiness and life. I said as much to Hector when I returned to my interrupted work, but he merely grunted, stretched, and went back to sleep. Under the paw he had moved was a toadlet I had missed.

Dogs are wonderful, but of limited imagination.

———————— • ————————

C ock blackbirds are fiercely competitive and territorial, even more so when they are breeding. If one joins my usual working companion (the one with a tiny white feather on his right cheek) each will purposefully hop towards his opponent, head down, yellow bill outstretched. One usually backs off. The victor unconcernedly carries on prospecting the lawn, his patch, for worms. He can carry several at once, and it always seems to be the cock who does most of the foraging for the young.

One of the shrubs by the side of the house had climbed up the drainpipe and was putting exploratory, tentative shoots round the gutter and under the tiles. I ought to have cut it back last autumn, but, well, it was one of those things that could wait, and now here we are with greenery everywhere and the last thing I want is a blocked gutter if a thunderstorm ends this hot spell. Out, therefore, with the ladder and the hedge trimmer and I set to work and clear off the first three or four feet. Ironically, as I start I think to myself, 'Well, by now any nestlings ought to be fledged.'

Just in time I see an eye bright like obsidian. The cutter bar stops inches from her head. Mrs Blackbird has sat tight through all the noise I have been making and the shaking of her home. Her right eye looks straight into mine. She is immobile, hunched down in her nice south-facing nest, orange bill pointing up at the sky. Her eggs must be very near to hatching for her to be so tenacious, and I hastily stop my job and go down the ladder.

But damage has already been done, for her nice sheltered nest is now in the full midday sun, and any watchful magpie or jay could see the nestlings when she is off the nest. I carry on working, at a job slightly quieter, keeping an eye on her – for I can see her bright eye and her bill from the ground. Then the bill is open, and I can see her tongue, as if she is panting in the heat. Poor thing! I felt dreadful, though any harm was wholly accidental, even if it all comes down to my fault for not finishing the thing off properly in the autumn.

What to do? Fortunately, she takes a break, and I can run up the ladder and erect a sort of canopy of the cut fronds and leaves where it will give her some shelter. I hope it works. And I hope it was not her mate whose corpse I found, dead a couple of days and already smelly, by the nearby dustbin. We shall see.

She did bring off her brood.

Along midsummer evening, with two candle lanterns lit on the table, and the quietening evening growing to dusk. The gibbous moon hangs over the roof ridge on its progress to the slow west. The swifts have ceased their curling circuits of the sky, still light high up above, and the staccato angularities of bats now crisscross the garden against the dying light in the north west. A bottle of wine to share with friends. Good talk, that goes everywhere and nowhere. One of us – we are all growing old – starts to talk of the faraway place he still calls home, though he has not been back for many years and will not now go again. It is obvious that his eyes are not seeing us, the candle light on our faces in the gloaming, but a bright sunlit morning of yesteryear. I know exactly what he feels: he is not telling us, though that is how he started, but reliving himself, the way he has come. He can be lyrical, for he has the gift of words. It's odd how when you least expect it, incidents, experiences, places, people of the long past are suddenly as present as if they were now. I wonder if this summer evening, and Bill talking, will be one of those involuntary vivid memories/time slippages that will colour the twilights of my own old age.

It certainly makes me think of my boyhood in the Crosscrake I so loved, where every day was summer, of the walk to school down the lane between the high hedges and the little wild red gooseberries in them that would be sweet and ripe about this time. Despite the solid breakfast at the vicarage, I was always already hungry again, and the half mile or so of lane provided earthy-smelling pig nuts – I had a penknife with which I could dig them up, and wiping them on my short grey worsted trousers would clean them enough – and gooseberries, and wild strawberries, and later there would be blackberries. As I passed the farm – the lane ran right through its buildings – there would be the smell of the milking, and the rich warm reek of the byre and the midden. At school at break there would be a gill of full cream milk in little bottles, and I hated being milk monitor because the crate in which the milk came smelt sour, and my hands smelt afterwards. Those smells – souring milk, dung, the pig nuts, the pink honeysuckle in the hedges – came back as fresh as yesterday when a lifetime later I walked with Hector the Labrador, just the two of us, along that strangely shorter road, where I could see over the hedges. He loved the smells too, though a dog's smell world is technicolour oil painting to our black line drawings.

Time, for once, on my hands, I had decided I would leave the car by the packhorse bridge at Stainton and walk through the well-remembered lanes and go a memory walk, up the Helm, where on the top of the ridge is a hill fort overlooking Kendal. It was late spring. The Helm is only a little hill, but it matters, for it is the first I ever climbed, ('because it was THERE') with Margaret. She was five years older than me, and had pigtails I never dared pull, and I thought the walk very steep and a very long way. I remember we had another Hector, Uncle Alec's and Auntie Gertie's (and Margaret's) white Scottie, with us, who ran ahead and started the odd rabbit out of shelter. He was too fat ever to have a chance of catching one. The late summer bracken was almost as high as my five-year-old head, and I could see a litter of old bracken from years before on the ground beneath the colonnade of the brown stems. I remember I was lagging and hot and grumpy, and then we came out to a sudden sight of all the kingdoms of the world, it seemed, spread out below us. (When Uncle

Alec preached on the Temptations, I imagined Jesus on The Helm looking down at Kendal and then turning to look over to the distant Irish Sea.) As the years passed and the clear domain of childhood receded into the blue rumour of memory, I drove past that hill many times on my way to somewhere else in cars far, far faster than the maroon and black Morris 8, and then the grey Morris E type, in which plump Auntie Gertie, blue straw hat pinned to the bun of her black hair streaked with lines of silver, drove her quiet little husband to meetings, singing hymns at the top of her considerable voice. He did not sing: he could intone the service, but, well, *bleated* in that once common Anglican manner.

As I said, time on my hands, and here I was going up The Helm again. No Margaret this time: she died young, long ago. The russet blanket of last years' dead bracken, flattened, its hard stiff stalks broken by the rains and winds of winter, looked only a very few weeks ago as if it would smother any new growth.

But look more closely. Here and there you can see the new fronds piercing the ground, insinuating themselves between the dead matter. Unnoticed beauty: for at every level, from the first uncurling of the tender shoot from the ground, to the tiny shoots on the growing stem to the full frond held in one last great curl before it spreads itself to the sun and rain, there is pattern and harmony. At every level the Universal Spiral, fractal upon fractal, all singing the mathematics of the pattern to which Leonardo Fibonacci gave his name, a spiral that links the shape and form of snail shells, of vortices in water, of uncurling fronds, to the Golden Ratio, and the harmonies of music. As Blake, that strange prophetic voice, said:

To see a World in a Grain of Sand
And a Heaven in a Wild Flower
Hold Infinity in the palm of your hand
And Eternity in an hour…

The only response is wonder. Mind you, bracken is an invasive nuisance, and its spores carcinogenic. One has to remind oneself…

We came out onto the long summit, into the light dappled by the scudding fair weather cumulus clouds that the fair wind was pushing off the sea. The hill fort is Iron Age, but certainly people used this hill long before that. The rampart and ditch make a sinuous circuit of the hill. Nobody there. There were larks, and a kestrel, the windhover, trod the wind before off, off, forth on swing to another station where the keen eyes could scan the ground for movement that might mean food. A rabbit excited Hector as it bolted into the nearby bracken. Hector looked at me expectantly: 'Please?' 'No,' I said firmly, and gave him a biscuit.

On the top I sat down, and looked over to the line of the Kent marked by the trees along its bank, and far over to the Lakeland hills beyond, blue with distance. Hector does not like it very much when I stop and sit down, and flumped down with a sigh beside me. It was easy to fall into a reverie, thinking about the people who built this fort. Is it something as simple as that, in fact, or something much more complex? I don't know. Perhaps they enjoyed being up here in the sun and wind as much as I realized I do, even had their place of assembly, possibly even of pilgrimage and worship, up here. (High places have always been special in European cultures, it seems: and in ancient Israel the Baalim had their ritual places on the tops of hills, but, says the Psalmist, in Psalm 121, damn all help came from *them*.[4]) They can't really have lived here for very long, with their animals, because, as with so many hill 'forts' (a word which begs many questions), there is no adequate supply of water. But as I began to doze, to go into what I call the mind's soft focus, I fancied – not for the first time – that I could hear the Old Ones' voices in the wind, that if I turned round I would see them, that they were not gone, that the place remembered them. But they were there. They called this place their own – if they had any concept of 'owning' things. And they were, unquestionably, our ancestors, our family.

———•———

That strange summer of 2020 made everyone realise how precarious were things we had always thought fixed, reliable. Those of us lucky enough to live outside the towns, with access to a bit of land on which to grow things, fared psychologically far better, I think. The routine of sowing, planting out, trimming and weeding insisted that there remained a rhythm in the year which could not be ignored, which was before man, which sustained him, and which would outlast his follies and

---

[4] I am going to be pedantic. St Jerome's translation of the Psalms into Latin made the opening 'Lev*avi* oculos', 'I lifted up my eyes unto the hills', which is firmly past tense, and one assumes he knew his Hebrew (a language where tenses are sometimes problematic anyway). Coverdale's English translation made it present: the Anglican Book of Common Prayer, despite quoting Jerome's Latin at the beginning, makes it future: 'I will lift up...' Which is why the psalm is so often part of the funeral services for hill walkers and climbers.

worries. Uneasy as I am about so many things, I have found that strangely comforting, and the garden has repaid the extra time not having to drive into town to do my work has given me to tend it.

Rarely if ever before have I had the garden looking so immaculate, the river bank grass trimmed, the vegetable garden full of plants promising abundance – though the gloomy countryman in me insists 'don't count your chickens, there's much can go wrong yet', for there is the first sign of potato blight. Even so, the greenhouse is full of luxuriating tomatoes with the first ones blushing red. This is one of the better consequences of a Coronavirus Lockdown, and Rosanna has taken the bit between her teeth, grown lots from seed as we could not go out and buy plants, and blessed us with thirty seven tomato plants of four varieties, a luxury of lettuce in three varieties and a bounty of beans of four varieties. I have never known a year so early, when things are so advanced. We are only just into July, and my early spuds – Arran Pilot, which suit this land – have yielded wonderful sweet tubers of exactly the right size. I have just lifted the last of them, for we have been digging them for a few weeks – again, as early as I can ever remember, for we started on them in mid May. Never have I had peas so early and so bountiful, the vines so laden with fruit that I hardly begrudge the odd pea moth caterpillar its guzzling of the peas inside the pod. We had some wonderful peas tonight, Onward variety. We gathered them together from the laden vines, and my Lady sweated them à la *française* with lettuce and garlic and a drop of oil. Wonderful. Grace was in order, and in abundance. 'For these and all His mercies…'

I have always got on with dogs, and they seem to like me. In fact, in years of walking round the village, with or without a dog of my own, I always seem to get the dog's name right, even if I cannot for the minute or two remember their owners'. I always have a few biscuits in my pocket, and my friends – not *all* get this treat – have come to know that, and will nuzzle my pocket if they can reach it. Rosanna will ask me, 'Who is so and so?' when I have just mentioned a name, and I will answer, 'Oh, that's Matilda's dad', or 'You know, she's Archie's mum.' Matilda, a Rhodesian Ridgeback bitch and Archie, a Border Collie dog, were two of my Hector's greatest friends. (Matilda would almost mug me for her treat.) When they got out of their own gardens, as they did, Archie being agile and Matilda having learned how to open the gate latch, they used to come and call for Hector. Matilda could look over the wall, round the tall gate, for all the world as if to say, 'Can Hector come out to play?' Archie would jump on top of the broad wall, and look: 'Is my friend there?' Just so Gunnar, the first Labrador, had a lifelong friendship – dogs do form friendships, as they do dislikes, just as we do – with a louche, smiley, lithe little cross-breed bitch called Brandy from the farm down the road. She too would call for him. As he was a big and powerful dog, he could jump the wall and off the two of them would go, and come back hours later, tired, happy, filthy – and as soon as he saw me, down would go his head and tail, as if to say, 'I shouldn't have done that, sorry, won't do it again.' But he did…

They leave a big hole in our lives, the dogs who have been your friends, when they go. They leave memories on a tree, a pond, a hillside, like their moulted hair on the floor, or on the sofa on which they were never allowed to sit: never the same again. Drummond, Sandy, Gunnar, Toby, and, last and dearest of them all, Hector – oddly, they all died in high summer, and the sunlight of July is always slightly clouded by that memory.

I remember the heartbreak in Gunnar's eyes, when I took the gun to go out for some pigeons in his last winter, unable to come with me because his back legs were failing. More than once I put the gun back and did not go. Hector's life as a working dog had been full and happy, and almost to the end he was active, though his kidneys were rapidly giving up and he was dependent on medication – which he took with a very bad grace. His sight was no longer keen, his hearing much worse, he could not walk far. But he would still make his way slowly to his favourite oak tree, read the doggy newspaper, inspect all the blades of grass on the way until he found exactly the right one for his squat or pee. Ten days before he died, knowing his days were very few, we took him back north to the shoot's annual summer barbecue and clay shoot. He was transported up to the ghyll he knew so well on the edge of the moor in a friend's Land Rover, for he could no longer manage that loved walk. He feasted on sausages, received with dignity the sniffs of his doggy friends, and during the shoot sat to attention, ears pricked, looking alertly around, mystified that there were no birds falling for him to pick up. Had there been, he could not have done it. Then, back home, he slept the last days away, lying on the sunny lawn. We gently moved him on his mattress into the shade as the day got hotter. He asked to sleep upstairs with us. We let him, though he had to be carried up and then down again. Finally the day came when I slept downstairs with him, woke up, heard his slow breathing next to me, and I knew that the vet had to come. He died with his head on my arm, and me stroking his silky ear for the last time. We scattered his ashes in his favourite pond down the fen, which he never passed without a swim. The big willows hang over the cool depths into which they slowly sank, briefly clouding the water. He is often there.

———•◦•———

August is when the year begins to look full, almost weary. Reeds along the river and in the ditches whisper that autumn is near. The droves are dry underfoot, the grasses coarse and with a tinge of brown, and spear thistles and burdock stand tall to flourish their purple flower heads to butterfly and bee. In the little open area in the wood there is a flourish of the delicate flat white flower heads of wild carrot, a one foot high top storey above the tiny jungle of grasses and hop trefoil, purple vetch and yarrow. In the sun those flat white polygons of wild carrot offer a feast to insects – fritillaries, a common blue, a black tipped soldier beetle, a large tortoiseshell, a red admiral. Soon thistledown will drift on the wind and goldfinches will feast, and burdock's hooked seeds will be fastening in animal fur, sticking on clothing as you brush past the spreading plant, to be discovered later miles from the parent plant – very efficient, and annoying, seed dispersal. The spring blue-green of the wheat has ripened to gold, and the ears have begun their ripening droop, and soon the combines will be busy chewing their way through the crop, excreting the crushed straw and dust as they go. Ripe wheat in hot sun has a very distinctive smell, bready without the whiff of yeast – once smelt, never forgotten, like the sicklier smell of a potato field. Once, the wheat stalks were much, much longer: a standing wheatfield came up to my thighs, whereas now it barely reaches my upper shins. Nobody wants the straw long any more. There is still some barley left to do: it had whitened to ripeness by mid July and usually, by this time of year, it would all be harvested. But we have had a couple of weeks when the showers kept on coming, and a little bit is still left. In the hot sun of this bright morning, and it looks settled for days to come, you can smell the damp of the earth, and the sweetish smell of wet vegetation. This sun is hot enough to burn off a lot of damp, and the barley pops and crackles as it dries. I met Bob Smith as he was walking out to his allotment, next to mine. 'I loves to hear that old barley pop like that', he says. He remembers mowing with a scythe all the long summer days of his youth, and would not wish those days back. Despite his 80 years, he'll be helping out on the combine later.

Insects everywhere. Horseflies home in on your smell, and settle unnoticed, silent, and knife their way into you. When you do feel it, it is too late. (But they do have beautiful eyes.) A peacock butterfly feeding on the burdock suddenly opens its wings, and its great eye markings glare at you. At home, on the vegetables and the roses, aphids are disappearing, gobbled up by the ladybirds and the few left are being tended by the busy ants running up and down the stems to collect the honey dew. Ladybirds, in fact, have been everywhere this summer, and they have found plenty of aphids and greenfly to gobble. Some summers, for reasons I don't know, we hardly see any ladybirds: perhaps they simply don't get through the winter. They vary from the little yellow ones with black spots to the ones after whom they named the books. They are welcome guests, for they chomp their way through aphids and greenfly by the score. Sometimes they hibernate in little clusters, under bark, in the folds of a tarpaulin, sometimes I find them even behind the grease rings I put on the apple trees. Their brightness in the cold of winter is a blessed reminder of the time when I shall be cursing aphids and greenfly, and I try not to disturb them, and around the garden now there are little structures in quiet corners, sheltered from rain, made of bits of canes or twigs, old fennel stalk, pine cones, laid horizontally side by side, into which insects can creep to hibernate. We saw a spectacular one in Nyon, in Switzerland, which gave us the idea. They called it an Insecthotel. It even had a roof like a Swiss chalet. If only one could guarantee that the refuge would be full of ladybirds…

For indeed I have had reason to curse greenfly, and blackfly, more than once. One year the blackfly got to the broad beans while I was away and so could not drench them with rhubarb water and washing-up liquid, and not a plant of a row which had been vigorous to a fault three weeks earlier survived. There was one very hot summer when the wind set easterly for days, gentle, hot, straight from Holland. I do not know what they had been doing in Holland, but we began to notice an unusual number of greenfly, increasing day by day. Soon the air was full of them, getting in eyes as you cycled, in hair, drowning in a cup of tea. They covered my vegetables. The swallows and martins and swifts were hardly bothering to fly, they were so full. Then yet more came, and gorged on the leaves of the trees, falling off, sated. The ground grew slippery, and under the beech and lime trees on the road cars left tracks as if through green snow. The ladybirds could not cope: their dinners just fell all round them, a plenty unimaginable.

My neighbour's little daughter – I speak of some years ago now – loved insects. She liked touching woodlice so that they curled up into a little grey balls which would roll about if you pushed them. But she especially loved ladybirds, and had them crawl up her to her raised fingertip so she could tell them to 'fly away home,/ Your house is on fire, your children's alone' – and they did, because they always believe you. Once she was peering intently at a pair on my gate post, rapt in copulation. 'Look, these two are married!' I agreed, of course. I gather that orgasm for the ladybird can last 40 minutes.

———•◦•———

When we first came to the village the combines were tiny compared with the monsters now that can cut a swathe 13 meters wide, thresh the grain from the ears and store 18,000 litres of the stuff. A few men, those in a small way, were still using reaper and binders. But most by then had got a red McCormick, which cut a swathe 6 feet wide, and delivered the threshed grain to a platform on which a man had to stand and hold a 2cwt sack to be filled, which was then tied and thrown off the back to be picked up later. And so on to the next. There were no airconditioned cabs with stereo, and driver and helper worked through the day in heat and clouds of dust and chaff. Yet it was less hard work than mowing by hand, or handling and stooking the tied sheaves from the reaper and binder. Men in a small way, and there were quite a few round here, continued to use those little old machines. That was before the world changed, before banks encouraged you to borrow money to buy what you could not afford (and then you had to work extra hard to pay off the loan and the interest), before their sons could not be doing with farm work and wanted jobs in the towns. Working on the combine *was* a hard, dirty job: I have done it, but it had its pleasures. Sometimes, the helper would have his loaded shotgun – most countrymen had shotguns – on the platform, and often you would get a shot at a hare or a rabbit as it bolted from the cut corn across the stubble to the safety of the edge of the field.

Then came the machines with grain tanks, and there was no platform from which to shoot. But the combine would still start at the headland at the edge of the field, chew its slow way round it, and gradually make a smaller and smaller island of corn in the middle. In there the game would slowly be concentrated. I can remember more than once being invited (I was delighted!) to 'follow the combine' as it swallowed ever more of the island, and if there were several of us we would stand around the field and most of us would take home a dinner. And then, perhaps, after the straw had been baled into those easily manageable rectangular bales that one man lifts with ease, came the primitive pleasure of firing what was left, and, days later, on the blackened lines where straw had been, the first shy mushrooms would peep out.

———••———

We had thunderstorms in Lancashire, but just as I don't think I had even noticed the aweful glory of the harvest moon until I came down here, so I don't think I had ever up there seen any thunderstorm to rival those that come shambling over from France or puff themselves up in the late summer thermals off this flat land. You can feel them coming: and just before they break often there is a stilling of the air, a quietening of the birds, a sudden breath of colder air, welcome in the heat, but you know what is coming and run around checking that drains and gutters are clear and putting tools away – and nowadays, switching off this machine. I can't compete with Emily Dickinson's poem:

The wind begun to rock the grass
With threatening tunes and low, —
He flung a menace at the earth,
A menace at the sky.
The leaves unhooked themselves from trees
And started all abroad;
The dust did scoop itself like hands
And throw away the road.
The wagons quickened on the streets,
The thunder hurried slow;
The lightning showed a yellow beak,
And then a livid claw.
The birds put up the bars to nests,
The cattle fled to barns;
There came one drop of giant rain,
And then, as if the hands
That held the dams had parted hold,
The waters wrecked the sky,
But overlooked my father's house,
Just quartering a tree.

And just as in Beethoven's Sixth Symphony, the sun comes out, the world is fresh and clean, and the birds sing again. The dust is laid, the drove has tiny flow patterns in its surface mud where the water rushed to find the ditch. The spider on the hawthorn unconcernedly visits her big web hanging between the wet shining leaves. That can stand most things. Except blundering men. She doesn't like males.

———————•———————

A rare pleasure this morning, despite the beginnings of a day of extreme heat already making a walk a sweaty and unpleasant business: on the path by the field beside the wood where the donkeys live, two bumble bees (*Bombus lapidarius*, I think) mating. I have never been lucky enough to see this before, and as the male is much smaller and differently coloured, if you saw them separately you might think them different species. She is bright, buxom, and tailed with flamboyant orange; he is half the size, more soberly tailed, and apparently goes around spreading little patches of pheromones to attract a lady. For some reason, the couple reminded me of those Donald McGill seaside postcards, sometimes risqué, featuring enormous ladies and their miniscule husbands, which on the way home from primary school I used to read slightly guiltily, pretending I wasn't, outside the Post Office. The bees' amour seems quite an energetic and long drawn out procedure. Then, still attached, they took off on what I would like to think was a mating flight to somewhere over the rainbow...

It just so happened that I was re-reading Gilbert's White's *Natural History of Selborne* during the Great Drought of 2018, and his description of the implacable, inescapable, heat of one June struck home. Connections: everything connects with everything else, everything affects everything else. If only we would remember that.

Example: on 8 June, 1783, Iceland burped. The eruption was in the craters of Laki, southwest of the Vatnajökull icecap. Scores of vents spilled out magma and poisonous gas. Between that June and the next February the eruption belched out more toxic gases than any eruption, anywhere, since. Iceland was devastated. But the toxic ash and sulphur dioxide cloud also drifted all over Europe. Rev. Gilbert White, writing to Daines Barrington from the soft midsummer Hampshire countryside at Selborne, said

'the peculiar haze or smoky fog was a most extraordinary appearance, unlike anything known within the memory of man… The sun, at noon, looked as blank as a clouded moon, and shed a rust-colored ferruginous light on the ground, and floors of rooms; but was particularly lurid and blood-colored at rising and setting. All the time the heat was so intense that butchers' meat could hardly be eaten on the day it was killed; and the flies swarmed so in the lanes and hedges that they rendered the horses half frantic, and riding irksome. The country people began to look with a superstitious awe, at the red, louring aspect of the sun…'

As well they might: people working outdoors choked as the sulphur dioxide reacted with moisture in their lungs to make sulphurous acid and their soft tissue swelled. The fog was so thick that boats stayed in port. The Indian and African monsoons failed, and the next few winters were savagely cold in America, Europe and Japan. The Nile flow was much lower than usual, and famine took about a sixth of Egypt's people in 1784. Everything, but everything, is interconnected: and I have given lectures on why Laki's explosive vomit was a major cause of the fall of the most secure throne in Europe – in 1783 – in the chaos of 1789. And everything that followed…

2018 saw no toxic cloud of volcano breath, but it was bad enough.

My diary tried to capture some of that unease I found impossible to shake off:

'Everyone old enough to remember the last big drought of 1976 brings out their stories of tinder-dry hedges and crops, of day upon day of baking temperatures and 52 days without rain. But this year feels different: this unremitting heat is beginning to feel sinister. Harvest, what there is of it, is earlier than I have ever known it. There are far fewer insects. Few butterflies sit and sun their wings on the remaining flowers. The car windscreen rarely needs the clean I used to have to give it to remove the splattered insects. The birds are hungry. The dwarf beans in the garden, usually such a mainstay, are poor thrawn things, dry before they are half grown, yellowing sere from their rich green long before their time. Grain is not the usual rich variety of browns, but bleached, almost white. Hard, parched earth shows through grass on lawns burned to a pale sepia, thin, like the few last hairs on an old man's head. Where people walk, the grass is worn away. Heat, heat, heat. There is real fear of fire grasping the acre upon acre of bone dry, standing corn. One discarded cigarette – and idiotic people do throw them out of car windows – or one malicious match, and a bit of wind, and the whole fen would be ablaze with the fire guzzling the corn and marching on the village. Lassitude... one cannot work well in this heat. Writing is done in little spurts, hoping I can remember the thought I had when I started this bit.

Down the Fen, gangs of men, Poles and Romanians, are lifting leeks and the allium smell drenches the stagnant air. Poor fellows, all day grilled under a pitiless sun, backs bent, and scant reward at the end. In Cambridge, pavements are full of tourists, mainly glum-looking Chinese, being taken on the obligatory trudge round the hot streets – the heat palpably beats up from the pavement – before being released to Shopping. Shops leave their doors wide, letting the cool air of the aircon spill out – how stupidly wasteful! – into the street to lure the customer in. The wiser of the homeless have set up their pitch to beg by those beckoning doors.

This morning I walked early across the wide usually green expanse of Parker's Piece and there was a carrion crow, open beaked, its pink tongue arched, panting. Black feathers take up the heat of the early morning sun. The low river is turgid with punts and splashing and noise. It smells. College lawns are brown, with no use for mowers. Fish gasp at the weir where the small tinkling dribbling fall – normally it is a smooth steady curve of bass-noted brightness in the sunlight – makes the water pick up at least some oxygen.

My blackbird – I have got to know him well during this nesting season, and a few weeks ago before the heat struck he used to follow me round waiting for the tasty morsel my spade or hoe would throw up – rests on the hoed garden where once it would find worms. Its wings are spread, its beak is open. As I dig deep for the last of this year's poor thin spuds, I turn up an earthworm, tightly and pinkly coiled into a little ball at the end of its hole. The thought strikes me, disturbingly, that a hundred years ago, when another man would have been digging potatoes for his family's winter from this land, he would have looked at this thin crop and thought, "We shall be hungry come Christmas." Snails aestivate, tightly stuck to each other in dark places where it might be cooler. Their epiphragmata are sometimes iridescent in the unwelcome light to which one lifts them. I put some down in the hope our thrush will find them. His song at twilight from the top of the ash tree has been deafening some evenings, carrying far down the Fen in this still air. Tired and moulting, a dusty blackbird, thin as a stick, does not budge when I approach. He is too weary to move away.'

'33 degrees today. The Fen is bone, bone dry. The apples are falling off the trees, and it is not yet August. Where the tractors are working on the peat Fen down by Dimmock's Cote great clouds of brown dust hang behind them in the still air. With any wind the Fen would blow – that is, there would be dust storms so dense the sun at noon would be the colour of a blood orange, drifts like black snow would form on the roads and in the ditches, and people would go about muffled. I have seen it so. Mercifully, the air is still, as it has been for days, though just occasionally a little dust devil will spiral up into the air, scooping up rattling dry leaves and bits of stem. The heat turns the horizon into a shiny turbulent sea.

'And silly people on the radio and in the papers say, "Aren't we having a lovely summer?" No: it smells of death.'

(Two days later):
'And then, the drought breaks: not as is usual with a rough, blunt, raucous, battering male thunderstorm, where the rain runs off the baked ground and does no good, but with two days of first gentle and wheedling drizzle, then serious constructive, feminine rain, that sinks into the ground and nurtures. What Chaucer calls a 'smoky' rain: I looked across the level fen, and saw the curtains of heavier rain billowing on the chivvying wind just like woodsmoke. The hot ground steams when the sun comes out.

'You could smell the rain coming – you always can after a long dry spell. It's a smell parfumiers would kill to be able reliably to reproduce and market. Fragrant oils from plants combine with a sort of alcohol made by actinobacteria, tiny organisms that make food for plants from dead or decaying matter. The human nose – not the most sensitive, and a joke when compared to a dog's – can detect just a few parts of that alcohol petrichor in a trillion of air molecules. The bugs go into overdrive when the ground moistens after a long dry spell in which their work of decomposition has almost shut down. Gratitude for such free gifts is in order.

'Slugs like young sausages, glistening in their new wetness, forage after their imposed fast. An immature moorhen lured by the wet grass – or where there was grass – finds itself in its long-striding, slow, foraging by the back door. And then notices that I am between it and its welcoming river. Panic. They looks so like their dinosaur ancestors when they run.'

A day later:
'Rain continues. There is the unfamiliar sound of rain on the roof of the lecture hall where I write this – for I am not listening to the lecture, so exciting is this rain.

I can see why in all cultures wells and springs and rivers have been honoured, why water was holy, a benison, a re-invigorating. By it we rise into new life, symbolically and in fact. But this sweet and lovely rain has come too late to save much of the veg crop. Nevertheless, my young leeks are now at last standing up straight, to attention, in their neat rows. Poor things, I kept them, our winter stay, alive, just, with what water there remained in the butts, but they never looked anything but round-shouldered, hollow-chested raw recruits.

'A tawny owl was calling down the fen when I went out with Hector the Labrador. Water drops from the tall sun-browned grasses his passage had stirred glistened on his fur in the moonlight.'

I am working very late. The door to the garden is open. Insects fly in, attracted by the light. A Yellow Underwing moth has settled on the mantelpiece. I am editing a book on Thomas Hardy's poetry, as it happens. He is an incomparable master of sound and pattern. I scroll to the next page, and I find my friend Neil by a happy coincidence is about to take his reader through an analysis of

An August Midnight

I

A shaded lamp and a waving blind,
And the beat of a clock from a distant floor:
On this scene enter—winged, horned, and spined—
A longlegs, a moth, and a dumbledore;
While 'mid my page there idly stands
A sleepy fly, that rubs its hands...

II

Thus meet we five, in this still place,
At this point of time, at this point in space.
—My guests besmear my new-penned line,
Or bang at the lamp and fall supine.
'God's humblest, they!' I muse. Yet why?
They know Earth-secrets that know not I.

To know Earth-secrets... That would be something.

This year, the Year of the Lockdown, the year the coronavirus insinuated itself into our systems so that nothing will ever be the same again, has been extraordinary in so many ways. That warm, dry, beautiful spring; the clarity of the unpolluted air; the quietness; those hard frosts in May; the extreme heat of early August, and now a big gale after thunderous rain. There has been a far greater number of migrant birds, and much more successful breeding of the raptors in the fen near us because people have not been around to disturb them. It seems to me there have been more insects, and more varied a selection – and more of that anon.

Then the crops have all been so early, earlier than I have even known, and so plentiful: a plethora of peas and a bounty of beans in early May, the last main crop spuds lifted in mid-August – not bad ones, actually, though not the best I have ever grown – and now the hawthorn berries are in their blood red glory in the hedges. Ripe blackberries load the bramble sprays – the best are always just out of reach, high up. The sprays nod in this big wind and revenge themselves on the incautious or unsteady picker who tries to steady them to rifle their bounty. Walnuts litter the ground.

Today dawned bright and noisy. I checked that the outdoor tomatoes were well staked before I set off down the Fen, eyes narrowed against the wind and the dust that was beginning to blow. Further down the drove, a recently planted hedge, now grown to about ten feet – the height when the old folk would be laying it – sheltered me from the wind. And suddenly, something I have never seen before: a host, (and I mean that word) of dragonflies hawking for prey all along in the lee, exactly as swallows do. They move pretty fast, though not with the flicker of swallows' flight, but occasionally stop dead in mid air, pausing as if about to go in to attack their victims – as indeed they often are. What made this sight especially memorable was the mixture of the biggest dragonflies this country offers – big, though far, far smaller than their ancestors in the Carboniferous period: several Brown Hawker (*Aeshna grandis*), Common Hawker, Southern Hawker (*Aeshna cyanea)*, and my favourites, the odd one of which Hodge the cat used to enjoy, Emperor (*Anax Imperator)*.

Scale is all. A dragonfly with a wingspan of 26 inches – well, if we had been around in the Carboniferous it would have been alarming enough. But the relentless predation of the modern pigmies is real enough to their victims, and their jaws fearsome. I was once lucky enough to see the kill. High on a path above Eskdale, going over to Wasdale one bright morning, the August bracken rose up to my waist and in the hot sun was alive with insects. I stopped to wipe my brow and bat away the annoying flies wanting a refreshing sip of my sweat, and sat for a moment on a convenient stone. A crane fly, quite newly hatched, was perched on a bracken frond, and my movement disturbed it. As it took off, out of nowhere a Brown Hawker zoomed in and took it on the wing in its big jaws, just like a peregrine taking a pigeon. Then it sat on the very frond which the crane fly had just left, and those jaws chomped its way through it. I could hear the crunch.

I have been here a long time. Many summers have come and gone. But some are unforgettable. I recall one early one, when we cannot have been here more than a couple of years, and still felt we were strangers learning a new country. It was a baking early September afternoon, the sky so pale blue it was almost white with heat. Absolute stillness. The sweetish smell of really hot ground, bone dry vegetation. Not a sound, not a soul about.

Old Seth, who had taken my rawness under his wing, and I are down on old Harold Sennett's land. (Sennett is an even bigger rogue than Seth. He keeps a punt hidden in the rushes on the lode bank so he can slip over into Wicken Fen Nature Reserve at dusk to knock off a few geese and ducks. As his father did before him.) Right down the fen, Harold's land is black peat, and there is a peat-digging, half-full of brown water, still in use by Seth and Harold. We have come down to pick up some ploughed-out bog-oak and some peats dried in a stack for Seth's fire. The black ground is hot to the feet; the reaper and binder has cut two swathes round a stand of wheat, and the eye is dazzled by the light reflecting off the exposed straight tall stalks of the standing crop. Not a breath sways those golden colonnades, soaring straight to meet above in the whiter tracery of ears. Yet Seth's sharp eye sees a movement near the centre of the block – no more than a few ears moving when everything else is still, and then stillness again.

'Old hare in there, like as not,' he says.

Out comes the gun from his sack; the damasked barrels clunk into the action, the fore-end snaps on. Two cartridges: as usual, nothing is left to chance, for these are the maximum load, virtually artillery strength. The gun is so old that the barrels are worn bright, the horns of the hammers – it has no safety-catch, of course – rubbed smooth by thumb pressure. Seth cocks it. Then, suddenly, for no reason apparently, he lowers it.

'Here. Dew yew take it. Jest yew walk round the edge of that old wheat and see if he don't put his head out.' He holds the gun out, still cocked.

I am dimly conscious that this is a challenge of some sort, and that it marks something of a watershed. I have never used a shotgun before. I have never killed anything except fish. I am unarguably about to commit several legal offences. And there is not a scrap of cover to hide me from anyone who might glance in this direction. If I hesitate, even, Seth's quick eye will notice; if I refuse, I probably lose a certain amount of growing trust, and I certainly will get a sneer. I might lose a friend. A refusal would certainly be told against me, and would be all over the village.

I take the gun. The metal already feels hot to the touch, and it bursts into light as the sun catches it. Seth reaches for his tobacco pouch. 'I'll stay here, head off that old hare from coming out.'

So off I go, gun at the high port as I have seen Seth carry it, praying that hare will have the sense to sit tight and not show its head out of the wall of wheat. One side. Now down the long side opposite Seth. Still no sign; but then, two-thirds of the way down, nicely in range, the corn starts moving: the hare is on the move. I freeze. Suddenly, at the base of the wall of dirty gold, there is the hare – just its head, its ears this way and that. But it sees me, and dives back into the wheat. I lower the gun, relieved, yet, somehow, deflated.

We did not get that hare. But in a sense honour had been satisfied, and Seth after that began to teach me more of the things that he had originally been secretive about. He taught me the difference (Oh, blessed difference!) between blackberries and dewberries; he told me the trick for shooting duck in all but the pitchiest of nights – chalk rubbed down the top rib of the gun. As the gun is levelled on the target the white line disappears. And he sold me his spare gun.

I had it for many years, a heavy old Gallyon side-by-side double hammer gun, made in Cambridge at the gunsmith's opposite the Round Church. Once upon a time I shot a good deal with it, but I stopped using it after I was thrown on my back by both barrels going off together. It was a rough old gun, indeed, and after Seth was dead I found out that it became his spare gun when he dropped it in the mud and a tractor ran over it. (That explained the home-made stock that had been fitted – not without some skill.)

Seth wasn't really doing me a favour in selling me that gun, and indeed, some would say he was taking advantage of my greenness. Yet I'm not sure. It was a safe enough gun to him, for years later I saw one of the best pigeon shots in the area using something far worse, with pitting in the barrels like a gravel workings. Seth knew I wanted a gun, that we had not got much money, and his price was just what I could afford. And the shivers that gun gives me now when I think what I did with it do not hide the keen memory of my bursting pride the first time I went out alone at dusk or dawn with it hidden in the lining of my coat. My gun.

And I did learn to shoot: to take advantage of the momentary glimpse of the quarry as it moved through cover, to be ever alert for a chance, to know the flightlines of pigeons or ducks, and to know the habits of pheasant and partridge – how for example in a frost they will on a morning move from cover onto bits of black earth or tarmac where one can wait for them. ('Their feet get cold, poor things', said Seth, 'and it's only kind to put them in the oven to warm them up.') I remember my first hare, shot with a gun I still have, a lovely little Belgian folding double-barrelled .410 that also fitted beautifully into the lining of a coat. A quick, clean kill, an unaccustomed heaviness in my jacket's capacious pocket as I walked home, the messy business of butchering soon over, and an extraordinary joy in the meals it provided. No meat ever tasted better than that, sauced with probably the most elementary pride known to man. And, recalling from my Northern childhood a farmer who cured his rabbit skins and used them for rugs and gloves, for years I kept that hare skin, pegged out, scraped and dried, to be the beginning of a bedside fur mat for daughter Antonia. But the moths got to it before I did. That was one of those things that never got made. There were so many...

***

My father's spade is bright with my use. Time and soil have worn it shorter. My son has Dad's Dutch hoe, and his own land to work. And after harvest comes another September, and my back aching from lifting spuds and the clear up of the garden after the summer, and another October, and picking the apples and storing them away from the ingenious and attentive mice. Dry leaves rustle in the lane as the wind blows them into little drifts, and they pile up by the hedge along the drove. Acorns litter the ground below the oak I planted. Soon there will be mud on my boots as the storms come from the west in the diminishing days before All Hallows' Eve, and then there will be Samhain fires to herald the coming winter. The cycle starts again. But a cycle is not a circle, endless repetition without meaning, for nothing is ever quite repeated. One year it's too dry, another too wet, one year the beans do well, another they are rubbish. It is rather a spiral, like a bean plant circling the pole that stays it from falling to climb to the light and its fullness of fruit. If autumn comes can our spring be far behind?

Our spring... one day every one of us will do what we see everything else doing all around us: let go. That is the one pattern the circling years teach. For without loss, no renewal, without death, no life. Everywhere in the life of the fields and woods, the seas and streams, the pattern is always that: death transformed, not death avoided. The universal spiritual pattern is death *and* resurrection, or loss *and* renewal, if you prefer. That is always a disappointment to us humans, because we always want the one without the other – transformation without cost, victory without, first, surrender.

I think there is something essential that we can only know by dying, and then we can't tell it. We really don't know what life is, what it is about, until we know what death is, just as we do not know how good a book is until we close it after the last page and it makes a whole shape. It seems as if the rhythm of death and rebirth is an essential part of how the cosmos works. Our sun itself was born out of death, the debris, the chaos, caused by the dying of an older star, and everything – every particle in our bodies, in our world – comes from that same sun that warms our backs as we dig in early spring, that ripens our fruit in autumn, that palely reminds us in midwinter of lazy summer evenings with friends and good talk and on the table the wine that the crushed grape gave us. Our sun will give up its own life, in time, to make something new. Something dies, something new is born: which is why, as some wise people I know say, the increasing chaos of our times – pandemic, economic chaos, climatic emergency, social upheaval – is, perhaps, a sign of hope, for in this travail something new is perhaps being born, a new way of engaging with the world of which we are a part, of which we are stewards not masters. Breakdown could be breakthrough if we recognize a new pattern of life struggling to emerge.

Yet it is still invariably a leap of trust, a walk into – and through – the darkness. No guarantees. The acorn might not germinate.

Acknowledgments

I have owed thanks to so many people in my long life, and I am not sure I always gave them as I should have done. For many it is now too late. But the making of this book is a thanksgiving for the life that has been vouchsafed to me in this place at this time. I owe gratitude beyond words to all those people in the hamlet who welcomed me as a stranger in my youth, as well as to those who now tolerate the eccentricities and garrulousness of my later years as I have become one of the Old Inhabitants.

But individuals have to be named. Of those no longer with us, Albert and Kate Johnson, and Seth Badcock, whose reproof and scorn my clumsiness feared but whose kindness taught me so much. Then there was Colin Washtell, my ingenious neighbour, passionate about history and music and bees and everything else, who taught me that every moment was for living. (That may be why I am now so unrestful a companion...) I owe more than words can say to my dear, dead Jenny, my first wife, with whom I shared so many of the hardships and happinesses of our early years in this place. To our children Antonia and Justin, with whom I could be young again in the morning of their world, I owe thanks and love beyond measure. But in the writing and completion of this book, how can I not give the humblest and heartiest thanks to my Rosanna Petra, very much alive, the love of my age, my wisest critic, my most generous friend.

CWRDM
Reach, Trinity Sunday, MMXXI

Further countryside reading from
Merlin Unwin Books

The Countryman's Bedside Book BB
The Naturalist's Bedside Book BB
The Best of BB
The Shootingman's Bedside Book BB
Sport in the Fields and Woods Richard Jefferies
The Way of a Countryman Ian Niall
My Animals and Other Family Phyllida Barstow
A Job for all Seasons Phyllida Barstow
The Sporting Gun's Bedside Companion Douglas Butler
The Poacher's Handbook Ian Niall
The Black Grouse Patrick Laurie
Geese! *Memoirs of a Wildfowler* Edward Miller
The Airgun Hunter's Year Ian Barnett
Advice from a Gamekeeper John Cowan
The Gamekeeper's Dog John Cowan
Nearest Earthly Place to Paradise Margaret Wilson
A String of Pearls Margaret Wilson & Helen Shaw
A Shropshire Lad A E Housman
Feathers: the game larder José Souto & Steve Lee
Venison: the game larder José Souto & Steve Lee
Much Ado About Mutton Bob Kennard

Wild Flowers of Britain Margaret Erskine Wilson

The Hare Jill Mason

The Rabbit Jill Mason

The Otter James Williams

Woodland Wild Flowers Alan Waterman

My Wood Stephen Dalton

Wildlife of the Pennine Hills Doug Kennedy

Hedgerow Medicine Julie Bruton-Seal & Matthew Seal

Wayside Medicine Julie Bruton-Seal & Matthew Seal

Extraordinary Villages Tony Francis

Myddle: *The Life and Times of a Shropshire Farmworker's Daughter* Helen Ebrey

Recollections of a Moorland Lad Richard Robinson

The WI Country Woman's Year 1960
Elizabeth Shirley Vaughan Paget

My Friends Who Don't Have Dogs Anna Levin

Available from all good bookshops
For full details of these books:
www.merlinunwin.co.uk